Prentice Hall Ser
in Advanced Business Cor.

D0143517

# Guide to

# Interpersonal Communication

*Joann Baney*
Professional Development Company
New York, NY

*Mary Munter*
Series Editor

PEARSON

Prentice
Hall

**Library of Congress Cataloging-in-Publication Data**

Baney, Joann.
  Guide to interpersonal communication / Joann Baney.
    p. cm.—(Prentice Hall series in advanced communication)
  Includes bibliographical references and index.
  ISBN 0-13-035217-9 (pbk. : alk. paper)
    1. Interpersonal communication. I. Title. II. Series.
  P94.7.B36 2003
  302.2—dc21                                    2003046391

*Acquisitions Editor:* David Parker
*Editor-in-Chief:* Jeff Shelstad
*Assistant Editor:* Ashley Keim
*Editorial Assistant:* Melissa Yu
*Executive Marketing Manager:* Shannon Moore
*Marketing Assistant:* Patrick Danzuso
*Senior Managing Editor (Production):* Judy Leale
*Production Assistant:* Joseph DeProspero
*Associate Director, Manufacturing:* Vincent Scelta
*Production Manager:* Arnold Vila
*Manufacturing Buyer:* Diane Peirano
*Cover Design:* Kiwi Design
*Cover Illustration/Photo:* Kiwi Design
*Composition/Full-Service Project Management:* Rainbow Graphics/Linda Begley

Credits and acknowledgments borrowed from other sources and reproduced, with permission, in this textbook appear on appropriate pages within text.

Pearson Education LTD.
Pearson Education Singapore, Pte. Ltd
Pearson Education, Canada, Ltd
Pearson Education–Japan

Pearson Education Australia PTY, Limited
Pearson Education North Asia Ltd
Pearson Educación de Mexico, S.A. de C.V.
Pearson Education Malaysia, Pte. Ltd

ISBN 0-13-035217-9

Dedicated to my treasures,
William and Joseph

# Contents

V **CHAPTER IV**

## SOCIAL STYLES  **44**

# PART II
# APPLICATION
# OPPORTUNITIES

**CHAPTER V**

## INTERVIEWING  **62**

**CHAPTER VI**

## NEGOTIATING  **80**

**CHAPTER VII**

## PERFORMANCE APPRAISALS  **94**

# Introduction

## HOW THIS BOOK CAN HELP YOU

This book can help you if you are looking to improve your interpersonal interactions in any business relationship. For example:

- You have been told you don't listen to people, but you don't know why they have that impression. What can you do differently?
- You need to deliver difficult feedback to a valued colleague. How can you do that without damaging the relationship?
- Although you spend significant amounts of time on the phone with clients, you never seem to gather the information you need. How can you ask questions differently to achieve better results?
- You want to improve your relationship with your boss but have a hard time feeling at ease. How can you adjust your behavior to create more comfortable interactions?
- You need to hire several new people to build your department. How can you approach the interviewing process to increase your chances of choosing the people with the best skills for the jobs, as opposed to the most comfortable conversationalists?
- You have to negotiate a new contract with a challenging vendor and feel intimidated by the idea. How can you prepare for the negotiation?
- You feel uncomfortable about conducting performance appraisals for your staff and are unsure about how to approach the interactions. How can you plan the sessions?
- You want to improve your business relationships and want ideas on how to manage your behavior to facilitate interactions.

- You want to evaluate your interpersonal skills in anticipation of professional advancement: how can you hit the ground running for more challenging interactions like interviews, negotiations, or conducting performance appraisals?

Read this book on its own, or use it as a reference when taking a professional course, college course, workshop, or seminar.

## WHO CAN USE THIS BOOK

This book is written for you if you want a guide for improving your business interactions and relationships. Specifically, the book will . . .

- Give practical advice on how to improve the foundational, interpersonal communication skills of listening, feedback, asking and responding to questions, and adjusting to another's style.
- Offer step-by-step recommendations for approaching common interactions like interviewing—from the perspective of both the interviewer and the interviewee—negotiating, and conducting performance appraisals.

## WHY THIS BOOK WAS WRITTEN

The thousands of participants in various management communication workshops and courses we have taught at universities and corporations in the United States and abroad have expressed interest in direct, step-by-step guidelines for interpersonal communication skills. They have found other texts in these areas too long, too theoretical, or too anecdotal for their needs. That's why Prentice Hall is publishing the Prentice Hall Series in Advanced Business Communication—brief, practical, reader-friendly guides for people who communicate in professional contexts. (See the inside front cover of this book for more information on the series.)

- *Brief:* This book summarizes key ideas only. Culling from thousands of pages of text and research, we have omitted bulky examples, cases, footnotes, exercises, and discussion questions.
- *Practical:* This book offers clear, straightforward tools you can use. It includes only information that you will find useful in a professional context.
- *Reader-friendly:* We have tried to provide an easy-to-skim format—using a direct, matter-of-fact, and nontheoretical tone.

# HOW THIS BOOK IS ORGANIZED

The book is divided into two parts.

## Part I: Building Blocks

Effective interpersonal communication is based on the building block skills of listening, feedback, questioning and responding, and awareness of others' styles.

**I. Listening:**   The cornerstone for building an interpersonal relationship is to listen effectively: using attending, following, and reflecting skills, and avoiding barriers to listening.

**II. Feedback:**   Delivering feedback can be a challenge. This chapter explains how to do it in a way that will help you to deliver feedback directly while maintaining your relationship with the other person. The chapter also gives tips on how to receive feedback from others.

**III. Questioning and Responding:**   How you ask questions can either encourage conversation or discourage long-windedness. This chapter reviews techniques for wording questions to elicit the kind of response you want, as well as how to respond effectively to questions.

**IV. Social Styles:**   Understanding how to identify and interact with people of different styles will help to improve your relationships. This chapter describes how to identify your own and others' styles, and gives tips on adjusting your behavior to facilitate interactions.

## Part II: Application Opportunities

This section applies the building block skills covered in Part I to three specific interactions in the business world: interviewing, negotiating, and conducting performance appraisals.

**V. Interviewing:**   This chapter covers the steps you follow in preparing for an interview, engaging in an interview, and following up after an interview—from the perspective of both the interviewer and the interviewee.

**VI. Negotiating:**   How to determine your strategy for a negotiation and how to conduct yourself during the negotiation for best results are covered in this chapter.

**VII. Performance Appraisals:**   Performance appraisals should be used as coaching opportunities whenever possible. This chapter covers how to prepare for a performance appraisal, and how to structure a session.

## ACKNOWLEDGMENTS

First and foremost, I would like to thank Lynn Russell, my longtime friend and business partner, whose ideas, enthusiasm, support, and exceptional talents made this book possible, make our business successful, and make work fun. Thanks also go to my many helpful colleagues including Grant Ackerman, Mike Fenlon, Tom Ference, Breanna Kirk, Bill Klepper, Lori Roth, Caroline Sherman, Virginia Weiler, Cheryl Wiles, and others who have provided feedback and insight into topics addressed in this book. I thank my husband, children, and all the Baneys and Bentleys for their assistance and support, and finally, thanks go to Mary Munter for her extraordinary talents, skills, and patience in editing this book and creating this series. I would also like to acknowledge the sources listed in the bibliography.

Joann Baney
Professional Development Company

# PART I

# *Building Blocks*

Several communication skills serve as the "building blocks" that form the base for all interpersonal communication. Improving your proficiency at these basic skills—listening, feedback, questioning, and awareness of style—will give you a solid foundation for developing your ability to interview, coach, negotiate, and manage. For example, you will negotiate better if you listen effectively—but how exactly do you listen effectively? You will coach others better if you deliver feedback effectively—but how do you deliver feedback effectively? In many cases, poor execution of these building block skills derails interpersonal exchanges. Part I covers these skills.

- **Chapter I:** What are the elements of effective listening?
- **Chapter II:** What is the best way to deliver and receive feedback?
- **Chapter III:** What are effective techniques for asking questions and responding to questions?
- **Chapter IV:** What are some ways to facilitate an interaction with someone who seems very different from you?

Developing proficiency with these communication building blocks involves work. Changing and improving the way you listen, deliver feedback, ask questions, or otherwise behave during an interaction can be challenging since adjusting old habits often feels awkward. However, enhancing your abilities at these basic skills will lead to improvements in more complex applications of these skills such as those discussed in Part II.

# CHAPTER I OUTLINE

I. Devote energy to listening
  1. Be aware of the benefits of listening
  2. Be willing to "learn to listen"

II. Practice active listening skills
  1. Use effective "attending skills"
  2. Maintain rapport by using "following skills"
  3. Practice "reflecting skills"

III. Avoid barriers to listening
  1. Avoid "judging responses"
  2. Refrain from "avoiding responses"
  3. Don't problem-solve

# CHAPTER I

## *Listening*

L istening is perhaps the most fundamental building block of interpersonal communication. Your ability to perform well at such tasks as interviewing a candidate, coaching an employee, or negotiating successfully depends to a large degree on your ability to listen effectively. Fortunately, listening is a skill that can be learned and improved with practice.

Listening is more than simply hearing. The first step in improving your listening skills is being willing to devote energy to listening. Second, effective listening requires learning and improving clusters of skills. Third, you need to avoid common conversational responses that derail effective listening. Awareness of these elements of listening behaviors, and adjusting your own behavior, will help you to improve your listening effectiveness.

## I. DEVOTE ENERGY TO LISTENING

For many people, effective communication means nothing more than talking in a persuasive and authoritative way: listening is often perceived as a passive, low-energy endeavor. However, listening effectively is not only integral to effective communication, it can also be a high-energy activity. As illustrated in the continuum below, listening can involve a range of energy. Listening to the radio or television is a low-energy listening activity. And in a group setting, like a classroom or a meeting, you can often fake attention and involvement, which makes these low-energy listening activities as well.

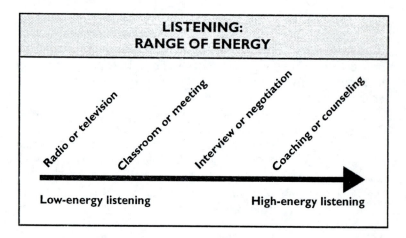

However, most business interactions—such as interviews, negotiations, or coaching sessions—require high-energy listening. To succeed in these types of interactions and respond to the subtle and spontaneous cues of interpersonal exchange, you need to be an active participant. Effective communication in these situations means engaging in high-energy listening. Your success in these interactions will affect your relationships and your career.

## 1. Be aware of the benefits of listening.

Why should you bother putting time and energy into listening to others? Because the interpersonal payoffs are so significant. People who have had someone listen to them intensely often report how powerful the experience was and how good they felt about the listener: the good feelings the speaker experiences when speaking freely and openly are associated with the listener who facilitates that expression. If you are looking to maintain or improve a relationship with someone, you need to listen.

### Listening is:

- *A critical communication skill:* In fact, the willingness and ability to listen has been identified as the single most important attribute of an effective manager. Since communication is a two-way interaction, as a listener you share the responsibility of how well someone is able to speak to you.

- *An important way to gather information:* Listeners learn. If knowledge is power, effective listeners can be powerful people. If you demonstrate a willingness to listen to others, you will learn many things of which you would otherwise be ignorant.

- *A path to business success:* Listening to someone can engender trust and goodwill, earn loyalty and respect, reduce interpersonal stress and tension, and promote cooperation. Listening will improve your relationships with just about everyone, and improved relationships will lead to greater professional and personal success.

## 2. Be willing to "learn to listen."

Studies show that we spend more time at work listening than any other kind of communicating. Of the time we spend communicating, 45 percent is spent listening, 30 percent is spent talking, 16 percent is spent reading, and 9 percent is spent writing. While most people underestimate their speaking abilities, most people overestimate their listening abilities: in fact, many professionals receive training to improve speaking and writing skills, but very few receive training to improve listening skills. However, listening is a communication skill that can be learned and improved. In many business scenarios, you will discover the need to engage in what is called "active listening."

**Empathize with the speaker.**   When listening actively, you must imagine how the speaker feels, and really try to care. You can't fake good active listening. Empathy—that is, active listening—requires you to be nonjudgmental and to seek clarification of feelings and information. If you aim to understand the experience and feeling from the speaker's perspective, many of the skills outlined on the following pages will come to you naturally. If you listen effectively to others, you can often help them to increase their own self-awareness or to approach and solve problems on their own.

**Control your responses.**   Knowing the nonverbal "look" of listening and having awareness of your own nonverbal patterns is important to your success. In addition, you need to control your emotions, especially the nonverbal display of your emotions. Be aware of your own biases in reaction to certain perspectives, characterizations, or words, and put off evaluating information until you have time to think it all through. Finally, pay attention to the speaker and the message, rather than allowing yourself to be distracted by ambient surroundings or by the speaker's less-than-perfect delivery. Effective nonverbal listening behavior is described under attending skills on pages 8–9.

**Expect listening to take time and energy.**   People who devote even a short time to experimenting with active listening report feeling tired after the experience. Listening with an open mind, free from judgment and defensiveness, takes time and is hard work.

## II. PRACTICE ACTIVE LISTENING SKILLS

The willingness to devote energy to listening is the start of doing it well. However, listening effectively also involves self-management. As a listener, you can process information at a much faster rate than a speaker can deliver it: people speak at a rate of approximately 130 words per minute, but you can process information at upwards of 300 words per minute. This gap means you have excess capacity for information and can drift into daydreams or think about unrelated ideas. To listen effectively, you need to control yourself and not drift away.

In his book *People Skills,* Robert Bolton describes active listening as being divided into three skill clusters, as shown in the framework below: (1) Display the outward signs of listening called "attending skills." (2) Encourage the other person to speak by exercising your "following skills." (3) Understand and summarize information by applying "reflecting skills."

| LISTENING SKILL CLUSTERS | |
|---|---|
| **Attending skills** | Your nonverbal behavior<br>Speaker's nonverbal behavior<br>Suitable environment |
| **Following skills** | Door openers<br>Minimal encouragers<br>Silence<br>Infrequent, directed questions |
| **Reflecting skills** | Paraphrasing<br>Making summative statements |

Adapted from R. Bolton, *People Skills*

## I. Use effective "attending skills."

The term "attending skills" refers to the nonverbal signals that indicate you are listening, as well as to your awareness of and sensitivity to the nonverbal behavior of the speaker. In other words, attending skills create the "look" of listening.

You can generally tell if someone looks as though he is listening to you. Similarly, other people can tell whether or not you look like you are listening to them. Since a crucial aspect of effective listening is encouraging the other person to speak by demonstrating that you value his contribution, looking like you are listening is a critical first step to successful one-to-one communication. In other words, it is not enough just to listen: you must also *look* like you are listening.

**Control your nonverbal behavior.**   You can demonstrate your interest in the following ways:

- *Maintain an involved posture.* Square your shoulders so you are directly facing the speaker; don't turn away or give him the "cold shoulder." If you are seated, lean forward slightly. Avoid fidgeting with hands, rings, pens, hair, or anything else. Avoid toe-tapping and shifting about. Move naturally in response to the speaker's movements.

- *Look at the speaker.* Don't bore a hole into her skull with unblinking intensity, but look into her eyes and at her face. In Western cultures, direct eye contact is an indication of trust. As a listener, looking away from the speaker more than about 20 percent of the time indicates lack of interest and involvement. By focusing on the speaker, you not only demonstrate interest, but also gain information by interpreting her nonverbal behavior.

**Consider the speaker's nonverbal behavior.**   A speaker's nonverbal behavior may contain important unspoken messages. As a good listener, you should be sensitive to the speaker's nonverbal behavior, as well as your own. Evaluate nonverbal behavior in the context of the speaker's everyday nonverbal behavior: if she always slouches in the chair, then that posture is not especially significant in any specific situation, but if she usually stands and sits erect, slouching is an important nonverbal to note. Pay attention to the following types of nonverbal cues:

- *Facial expression:* Does the speaker look happy, excited, angry, worried, or sad? Are her expressions animated or still?
- *Eye expression and contact:* Do the speaker's eyes sparkle, narrow, cloud, or tear up? Is she making direct eye contact with you, or looking away?
- *Body posture:* Is the speaker alert and upright or slumped and slouched? Does he appear confident, energized, defeated, or apathetic?
- *Gesturing pattern:* Is the speaker gesturing a lot or a little? Are his gestures large or small? Is he gesturing in a relaxed, comfortable way—or nervously biting nails, tapping fingers, and so on?
- *Vocal expression:* Listen for changes in volume, inflection, and pace, or other patterns like lengthy pausing or stammering. Does she sound shocked, excited, embarrassed, unhappy, and so on?

**Choose a suitable environment.**   In anticipation of a one-to-one interaction where you want to listen well, choose an environment that will allow you to devote your attention to the speaker.

- *Eliminate distractions.* Choose a setting free from distracting phones, computers, beepers, or interlopers. Close your office door and shut down modern conveniences that demand immediate attention. These interruptions will distract you and possibly derail the speaker.
- *Consider the space arrangement,* and choose one suitable to the purpose of your interaction. For example, for informal exchanges, or ones in which you want to build camaraderie, choose a setting without the barriers of desks or tables between you and the speaker. For formal exchanges, where you want to communicate authority, you may choose to sit behind your desk. Also, consider the distance between you and the speaker and choose one that will feel most comfortable. Anthropologist Edward Hall divides space between people into four different zones: intimate (0–18″), personal (18″–4′), social (4′–12′), and public (over 12′). Most business conversations in the United States take place in the personal or social zones.

## 2. Maintain rapport by using "following skills."

"Following skills" go beyond the "look" of listening. Following skills prompt and encourage the speaker. They include opening an interaction in a way that helps make the other person feel comfortable, and using nonverbal and verbal encouragement to prompt the speaker to continue talking. Balancing verbal encouragement and silence is one of the major challenges of effective following. Work to use a combination of the skills discussed below.

**Open the door.**   "Door openers" let the speaker know you are ready and willing to listen. When you open the door to a listening session, your goal is to let the other person know you would like him to share what is on his mind.

- *What to do verbally:* Most door openers are brief statements or questions that are open and welcoming in nature. "Hey, what's up?" "Want to talk?" "You're looking like something's going on with you," and "Tell me about it" are examples of verbal door openers that might initiate an informal conversation. More formal interactions, like negotiations, performance appraisals, or interviews, might call for more direct or specific door openers like: "Let's talk about your goals. I want to hear your thoughts," or "Tell me about your background."

- *What to do nonverbally:* A nonverbal door opener might be gesturing toward a seat and making eye contact to indicate your willingness to listen.

- *What to avoid:* Watch out for door closers that shut down communication, such as criticizing or diverting attention back to yourself. When you open the door to a listening session, your goal is to let the other person share what is on his mind.

**Use minimal encouragers.**   "Minimal encouragers" are verbal or nonverbal signals that you are paying attention and following the logical sense and emotional content of the speaker's message. For some people, verbal encouragement demonstrates true support for the speaker, and some speakers rely on this interactivity to bolster their energy to continue speaking.

- *What to do:* Typical nonverbal minimal encouragers are smiles, nods, raising eyebrows at surprising news, frowning sympathetically at disturbing information, and otherwise demonstrating understanding of the message through facial expression. A verbal minimal encourager can be a simple "uh-huh," or a rhetorical reaction to information, such as "Really!"; "I see what you mean"; or "Wow!"

- *What to avoid:* Although you want to encourage the speaker, you should aim at avoiding a situation where the interaction becomes about your reaction to the message, such as how shocked you might be at certain information. A listener's job is to enable and facilitate the expression of the speaker, not to be a diversion.

**Be silent.** As obvious as it might seem, one of the biggest challenges for many listeners is just being quiet and letting the other person talk. An active listening scenario is not the same as a casual conversation where you might feel free to jump in at any time. Instead, you need to be quiet sometimes. Don't take control of the interaction by interrupting with personal reflections or war stories. Attend to the other person's style and pace, and give him time to continue. Wait. Let the other person talk.

**Ask infrequent, follow-up questions.** Sometimes the speaker needs more follow-up questions to sense your interest. Knowing when to interject with a question without usurping control is tough, but if the speaker seems stalled or focused on your reaction, you might encourage him by asking a question like: "So, then what happened?" or "What was that like?" Try to keep questions relevant to the speaker's content and feelings; don't interrogate for your own purposes.

### 3. Practice "reflecting skills."

"Reflecting skills" allow you to check whether or not you accurately heard the messages the speaker is trying to deliver. Reflecting skills are the listener's way of clarifying and summarizing the speaker's messages. This is your opportunity to demonstrate to the speaker that you heard her message by doing the following:

## Paraphrasing:

- *What it is:* A paraphrase is a brief restatement of the speaker's comments using your own words. How a speaker describes a situation sometimes only approximates her thoughts or feelings about it; paraphrasing helps to clarify the speaker's message for both the speaker and the listener.

- *Why do it:* To some people, paraphrasing seems awkward or irrelevant: why should I repeat what someone just told me? As a listener, your goal for paraphrasing is to understand the speaker's meaning and "get it right." Paraphrasing clarifies your understanding of the speaker's message and demonstrates to the speaker that you care. In addition, paraphrasing helps you to identify and retain key information which might be factual or emotional, stated directly or merely implied.

- *How to do it:* When paraphrasing, try to read between the lines and get a sense of the overall message. You might begin a paraphrase by identifying the speaker's main message from a lot of detail: as an example, "So, it sounds like you are really happy about your last meeting with that client. Is that right?" If this is an accurate paraphrase of the speaker's message, she can so indicate that and move on; if it is inaccurate or incomplete, she can clarify or expand.

**Make summary statements.**   Learning to paraphrase well will also help you to create summary statements.

- *What it is:* A summary statement can be several sentences that encapsulate past paraphrases and pull them together for a big-picture paraphrase. Such a statement might point out consistent themes advanced by the speaker. Don't use a summary statement to challenge the speaker or cause defensiveness: you are not trying to expose flaws in the speaker's perception or judgment; rather, a summary statement is meant to mirror back the speaker's comments: "So, all in all, this is what I heard you say."

- *Why do it:* You can help someone better understand her own thoughts and feelings by summarizing what you heard her say. An effective summary statement might enable the speaker to recognize themes or consistencies in her own thoughts. A summary statement can help people see their own concerns more clearly.

## III. AVOID BARRIERS TO LISTENING

Listening barriers are responses that inhibit the speaker from communicating further. In ordinary conversation, these barriers might not prove to be much of an impediment; but in situations where you are trying to listen actively, some responses create barriers that can defeat your listening objectives. Robert Bolton describes three types of barriers to listening—judging, avoiding, and problem-solving—as shown in the figure below.

| BARRIERS TO ACTIVE LISTENING | |
|---|---|
| **Judging responses** | Criticizing<br>Praising<br>Diagnosing<br>Name-calling |
| **Avoiding responses** | Diverting<br>Using logical arguments<br>Reassuring |
| **Problem-solving responses** | Giving advice<br>Ordering or threatening<br>Questioning excessively |
| | Adapted from R. Bolton, *People Skills* |

Do you use any of these listening barriers? After reading through this section, ask people close to you for feedback about the responses you give when listening, or listen to your own comments in your next few conversations. Then, consider what behaviors you could use instead of these barrier responses, to return to the elements of active listening.

## 1. Avoid "judging responses."

"Judging responses" arise from the natural tendency of listeners to share their own reactions and views with speakers. There is a time and place for some judging responses, but not while you are listening actively. Once you have made a judging response, the speaker can't continue without factoring in your now-stated perspective: the speaker must shape his comments to accommodate your view.

For the next few examples, imagine a staff member has told you about a project he has been working on which has been fraught with technical problems due to a newly installed computer network. In an active listening situation, avoid any of the following types of judging responses.

**Criticizing:**   "You haven't done much of a job of thinking this thing through." Criticizing will probably create defensiveness in the speaker. The speaker will not only probably resent and remember the criticism, but he may also try to counter the criticism or decide to end the interaction.

**Praising:**   "You always manage to have things work out brilliantly, so I bet you'll soon know more about the network than anyone." Criticizing seems like a more obvious door closer, while, on the surface, praising doesn't seem like such a bad thing because praising someone is usually motivating. In active listening situations, however, praising may dismiss or ignore someone's concerns: the speaker may feel you do not want to be bothered with any details.

**Diagnosing:**   Telling someone about his personality flaws will probably cause defensiveness or challenge his self-esteem. For example, "Your problem is that you aren't comfortable with new challenges." With a diagnosing response, the speaker's character is now the topic of conversation, instead of the topic she introduced.

**Name-calling:**   "You're such a technophobe!" If you make a name-calling response, the subsequent conversation will focus on the ramifications of the name, instead of on the issue the speaker would like to discuss. Name-calling may cause resentment and end the conversation as well as damage the relationship.

## 2. Refrain from "avoiding responses."

The second set of impediments to listening involves avoiding the speaker's concerns by changing the subject. These responses either shift the topic to one of the listener's choice or end the interaction completely. For example, if a staff member is telling you about a project fraught with technical problems, you should refrain from the following responses.

**Diverting:** "That reminds me of a project I was working on last year. Let me tell you how bad that was. . . ." Diverting moves attention away from the speaker's concerns and toward the listener's anecdote. Listeners may think that these kinds of diverting responses will bolster the speaker's confidence by demonstrating that everyone experiences difficulties and challenges. However, diverting simply upstages the speaker.

**Using logical arguments:** "The computer system had to be upgraded for us to stay competitive, and you may as well learn to use it sometime." Logical arguments negate the emotional perspective of the speaker. While the logic might be sound, it does not allow for the speaker's feelings, which may represent the speaker's central message.

**Reassuring:** "Don't worry about it. It will all work out fine." Although you may feel you are being helpful, reassuring dismisses the speaker's comments as petty, needless worrying—and is a typical way to try to end a conversation.

## 3. Don't problem-solve.

When you are listening, avoid offering unsolicited advice or a quick-fix solution. Businesspeople are often problem-solvers and are tempted to jump in and tell others what to do. Let the speaker describe her experience and resist the temptation to give her "the answer." Problem-solving is ineffective because (1) you may jump in too soon with a solution without uncovering the real problems, (2) the speaker may want empathetic listening and not a solution, and (3) many times a person can develop her own solution to a problem if given the opportunity. Problem-solving is especially ineffective when someone is facing an interpersonal challenge because successful solutions to interpersonal challenges are usually dependent on an individual's style and comfort: what might feel like the right course of action to you might feel impossible to the other person. Avoid responding with the following solutions.

**Giving advice:** "I know just what you should do. . . ." In many cases volunteering advice is insulting because it implies you can figure out in a moment and with limited details what might have been troubling the speaker for a long time. Many times people can figure out what is best for them if you allow them to speak: refrain from giving advice unless you are asked.

**Ordering or threatening:** "You just better fix it right now," or "If you don't figure it out, I'll have to bring in a consultant and that won't look good for you." This type of response almost guarantees that the speaker will not approach you again with other concerns.

**Questioning excessively:** "When did the first problem occur? Did you report it immediately? How many problems have you had altogether? How much have the problems cost in overtime?" Questioning excessively puts the listener, not the speaker, in control of the information.

---

In summary, you will improve your business and interpersonal effectiveness by developing your listening skills. If you try to truly understand the perspective of the other person, most of the components of active listening will come naturally to you. Practice the active listening skills of attending, following, and reflecting, and avoid barriers to listening such as judging, avoiding, and problem-solving responses that shut down the speaker and discourage communication.

Most importantly, recognize that listening is not a passive endeavor; rather, as a listener, you are an active participant in a dialogue and your listening effectiveness can actually encourage another person to speak genuinely and thoughtfully. Not every interaction will require you to listen actively. However, developing and perfecting your active listening skills gives you the flexibility to use them when the situation calls for it. If you are known as someone who will listen, you will learn many things about people's interests and concerns and understand what motivates or inspires them. This will improve your effectiveness as a businessperson, colleague, and friend.

# CHAPTER II OUTLINE

   I. Understanding good feedback

  II. Constructing feedback messages
      1. Use a three-part message
      2. Deliver your message, then listen

 III. Receiving feedback constructively
      1. Consider how feedback increases self-awareness
      2. Follow tips for receiving feedback

# CHAPTER II

# *Feedback*

Just as listening effectively entails more than simply hearing, delivering feedback effectively entails more than simply reacting with your opinion. Effective feedback is a combination of describing behavior and its consequences and motivating another person. Giving feedback effectively is an essential and unavoidable part of interpersonal communication and is critical to your success in professional and personal relationships. In addition, a willingness and ability to receive feedback from others is key to improving job performance and relationships.

You can improve a relationship by motivating someone to make changes in her behavior that may enhance her productivity or effectiveness, or improve her relationships. In negative situations, delivering feedback effectively minimizes the chance the behavior will recur. In positive situations, it maximizes the chance the behavior will be repeated. You can listen to others' feedback and make changes in your own behavior and possibly experience the same benefits. The challenge is to deliver and receive feedback constructively.

# I. UNDERSTANDING GOOD FEEDBACK

Effective feedback motivates someone to repeat positive behavior or discontinue negative behavior. According to organizational behavior expert Chris Argyris, if feedback is delivered in a threatening way, it will increase defensiveness and reduce the probability of learning, or changing. Therefore, before you can deliver feedback effectively, you need to begin with a commitment to treat the other person with dignity and respect. Then keep in mind the characteristics of effective feedback that communication expert Lynn Russell describes with the mnemonic "SAY THIS."

---

### "SAY THIS"
### MNEMONIC FOR FEEDBACK

**S**pecific and descriptive
**A**bout behavior that can be changed
**Y**ours—so own it

**T**imed appropriately
**H**abitually two-way
**I**ncremental
**S**upportive, as well as constructive

*SOURCE:* L. Russell, Professional Development Company

---

**S = Specific and descriptive:**   Effective feedback is specific and describes observable behavior.

- *Specific:* Specific feedback is free of generalizations such as, "You are always disorganized," or "You are never on time." Instead, focus on a particular instance of behavior such as, "You have not organized this client file," or "You are 25 minutes late." Specific instances of behavior are easier to consider and address. Additionally, there is usually an exception to any generalization, making it easy to dismiss or contradict such statements.

- *Descriptive:* Describe the person's behavior objectively. Don't guess at reasons or motivations. For example, instead of saying "You don't care about being on time," or "You resent your early morning office responsibilities," you might say "You were scheduled to arrive at 9:00 this morning, but you arrived at 9:40."

**A = About behavior that can be changed:**   Since your aim in delivering feedback is to change behavior, make sure you are addressing behavior that *can* be changed. You can't change someone's personality, so choose a specific behavior that can be changed instead. For example, you can't stop someone from being talkative and gregarious, but you can get them to stop gathering groups for coffee breaks in the reception area.

**Y = Yours—so own it:**   Take responsibility for your viewpoint. Stick with your own observations and reactions as much as possible so you can always defend what you are asserting. Delivering other people's feedback is usually a bad idea. If you are representing other people's perceptions, you may have a difficult time pointing to specifics you didn't witness, and might create worse feelings between the people involved, instead of helping matters. Also, feedback that begins with phrases like "everyone thinks" or "they all told me that" usually makes the recipients feel that everyone talks about them behind their backs.

**T = Timed appropriately:**   Delivering timely feedback is important. Timing the delivery of feedback not only relates to scheduling convenience, but also to your state of mind and the state of mind of the person hearing the feedback.

- *Deliver feedback within one or two days of an event.* Don't wait three months to tell someone about her behavior, when it may be too late to make any changes. On the other hand, immediate feedback may not always be the best course of action. For example, if you are angry, wait long enough to allow your anger to cool so it will not interfere with the delivery of your message. Also, if the other person's self-esteem is low, you should wait for a better time. Barring extreme circumstances, however, most feedback should be delivered within one or two days.

- *Wait until you can deliver feedback privately.* Don't deliver feedback in public or if anyone is nearby and may overhear you. Although a quick compliment in public is usually appreciated, giving detailed feedback (negative or positive) in front of other people usually makes the other person feel uncomfortable about being publicly assessed.

- *Check your motivations.* Make sure that personal circumstances do not interfere with your giving feedback. Don't deliver feedback if your hidden agenda is to show off how much better you are at something. In these cases, the motivation is wrong, so the timing is wrong, especially if you are planning to send a hard-to-hear message.

- *Don't hit and run.* Be sure you are willing to hear a reaction to the feedback you deliver and that you both have enough time for a conversation about it.

**H = Habitually two-way:**   If you want to deliver feedback in the most effective way, be open to receiving it as well. Encourage others to give you feedback by letting them know you are looking to improve your performance or understand your behavior. Ideally, by delivering and receiving feedback effectively, you will encourage others to do the same.

**I = Incremental:**   Don't overwhelm anyone by dumping too much feedback all at once. If people receive too much feedback at one time, they may feel overwhelmed and miss your most important point amidst all the others. Instead, plan and limit your messages.

**S = Supportive as well as constructive:**   If people only hear negative comments from you, they may dismiss you as a crank that is always looking to criticize. Therefore, if you want people to listen to constructive feedback, you need to balance it by sharing positive feedback as well: "catch them doing something good" and say something. General praise for a job well done and general compliments are not enough: you should also be specific and descriptive with your comments.

## II. CONSTRUCTING FEEDBACK MESSAGES

Using "three-part messages" described in this section will ensure that you incorporate the seven characteristics of good feedback covered in the previous section. Effective feedback messages enable you to clearly identify behavior and minimize the interpersonal tension, resentment, and defensiveness that delivering feedback can often create.

In this section, we'll use the example that a work colleague always seems to interrupt you in meetings. You may imagine that she thinks what she has to say is more important than what you have to say, or that she likes to hear the sound of her own voice. Instead of sharing these kinds of implied motivations or negative thoughts, consider using the following three-part message.

| ASSERTIVE FEEDBACK: THREE-PART MESSAGE | |
|---|---|
| 1."When you ..." | Objectively describe the behavior |
| 2."... I feel/am ..." | Identify your response |
| 3."... because ..." | Explain impact of behavior |

Adapted from R. Bolton, *People Skills*

### 1. Use a three-part message.

**Objectively describe the behavior.** Before you deliver your message, identify the behavior you would like to address. Since you want to maintain a good relationship with the other person, describe the behavior as objectively and nonjudgmentally as possible so that you can motivate the person to change the behavior rather than offending or insulting him. Start the message with the phrase "When you ... ": "When you arrive at the office at 9:25," instead of "When you goof around on your way to work"; "When you do not submit documentation for office purchases," instead of "When you think no one keeps track of the budget around here"; or "When you do not prepare an agenda for a new client meeting," instead of "When you think you

are good enough to just wing it" are examples of objective, nonjudgmental descriptions of behavior versus comments that might offend
or insult. Keep the following guidelines in mind as you develop this
part of the message:

- *Don't guess at motivations.* For example, the phrase "When you think
  that what you have to say is more important than what anyone else has
  to say" does not describe observable behavior. Rather, it assumes you
  know what the other person is thinking. You don't.

- *Don't generalize.* For example, "When you constantly interrupt me at
  meetings" contains the generalization "constantly." Since the interruptions can't possibly be constant, he might divert the feedback conversation to give examples of when he didn't interrupt you. In addition, people tend to dismiss generalizations as unfair exaggerations.

- *Don't use loaded language.* In this case, the word "interrupt" is
  loaded with judgment. Since most people recognize that interrupting
  is rude behavior, saying that someone interrupts is the equivalent of
  saying he is rude. Instead, try to come up with an objective, nonjudgmental description of the behavior, such as, "When you begin speaking before I finish speaking. . . ."

**Identify your own response.**   Once you have described the other
person's behavior ("When you. . . "), own up to your own reactions
or feelings generated by this behavior by using the phrase "I feel" or
"I am."

- *Consider a reasonable reaction to the situation.* If you have been letting someone interrupt you for years and never addressed it, you
  might feel like you are about to explode with anger. It is not the other
  person's fault you have never tried to address this issue before. He
  may be completely unaware that he has been doing anything to irritate
  you. He might even be under the impression that he has been helping
  you get your points across by enthusiastically adding to your comments before you have finished speaking. Therefore, try to avoid an
  extreme or excessive reaction, and identify what is reasonable in
  response to the most recent example of his behavior.

- *Use the right "feeling word."* Examples of effective "feeling words"
  in this situation might include "frustrated","irritated", "bothered", or
  "annoyed". Don't turn this part of the message into a guess at the
  other person's motivation, however, as in "I feel like you don't respect
  me," or "I feel like you don't value my contributions." Instead, identify your own feeling. If mentioning feelings is uncomfortable for

you, you might just say "I don't like it," or decide to keep feelings out of it altogether, and continue to the next step.

**Explain the impact of the behavior.** The third part of your message should explain the impact of the behavior using the word "because. . . ." Be certain the impact you describe is legitimate, realistic, and nonjudgmental.

- *Point out a tangible impact.* If possible, try to identify a tangible or work-related impact. For example, "I lose my train of thought," or "I need to restate my points to clarify my message."
- *Tie the impact to the other person's needs, too.* Consider the perspective of the other person. Identifying an impact that has particular significance to the other person can be helpful, so keeping in mind his style, goals, and objectives can help you construct the third part of the message to make it especially meaningful to him. For example, perhaps you know that he likes meetings to end on time. If so, you could say "because our meetings are less efficient and take longer."
- *Consider the other person's feelings.* Some people will be very surprised to learn they have been doing something that bothers you. For them, this third part of the message might not even be necessary: letting them know you are bothered may be enough for them to want to change their behavior.

**Combine the three parts of the message.** Putting together the three parts of the message means you will be saying something along these lines: "When you begin speaking before I finish speaking, I feel annoyed because I can't complete my thought." You may also switch the order of the three parts of the message: "I don't like it when you begin speaking before I finish speaking because I can't complete my thought," or, "I can't complete my thought when you begin speaking before I finish, and that bothers me." If mentioning your feelings is uncomfortable for you in this situation, you can leave that part out: "When you begin speaking before I finish speaking, I lose my train of thought."

**Deliver positive three-part messages as well.** The three-part message structure is not only an effective way to discourage negative behaviors; it is also a useful technique for acknowledging positive behavior. Using a three-part message to validate behavior has several benefits: it is helpful for people to understand specific details of their good performance and the effects of that performance, and for them to hear about how people feel about the behavior. Practice the three-part message structure with positive, supportive messages like: "I like it when you come to meetings at the scheduled time, because we can hope to finish on time," or, "When you prepare an agenda for client meetings, I feel confident that we won't forget anything important." Practicing with positive messages will make constructing and delivering difficult messages easier because the pattern will be familiar to you. In addition, if people hear positive messages from you, they will be more inclined to listen to more difficult messages: you will build your credibility as being fair and balanced.

## 2. Deliver your message, then listen.

Once you have constructed your three-part message, you need to deliver it effectively.

**Deliver your message.** Your nonverbal delivery of the message will affect its impact and effectiveness. Visualize calmly delivering the message and effectively managing the subsequent interaction. Practice your message aloud, or say it in front of a mirror. Asking someone to help you to role-play a rehearsal of a particularly important message or exchange—like delivering feedback to your boss or a problem employee—can also be helpful. Practicing will help you feel calmer and more in control.

- *Posture and gestures:* Maintain an open posture, squarely facing the other person with your feet planted, and head level. Use natural, emphatic gestures to reinforce your message.

- *Eye contact and facial expression:* Look directly at the other person with a serious, purposeful expression.

- *Voice:* Take a slow, deep breath before you begin; speak in calm, even tones at a conversational volume.

**Listen to the other person's response to feedback.** Even if you deliver a perfectly constructed message, you will create some interpersonal tension. As uncomfortable as it might feel, you need to allow time for the other person's reaction. Shift into active listening. Don't allow yourself to be sidetracked by baiting, counterattacks, or diverting questions. Respond calmly and respectfully to diminish possible escalation. In some cases, a person receiving feedback may respond by raising his voice in anger, or even begin to cry. You should try to respond to those reactions using the "reflecting skills" of active listening on pages 11–12, such as, "Hearing this is upsetting to you," or "You don't like hearing what I am saying to you right now." If a person responds defensively to a well-constructed message, she may not have heard the message clearly or understood it from your point of view.

**Repeat your message (if necessary).** If a person responds by denying or dismissing your feedback or by changing the subject, you may need to restate your message. After the person is finished speaking, calmly deliver the message again, perhaps more than once, each time allowing for the person's reaction with listening and reflective responses. Be persistent: stick with the message you developed for this interaction. Resist the temptation to escalate demands. For example:

| | |
|---|---|
| You: | When you begin speaking before I finish speaking, I feel frustrated because I can't complete my thought. |
| Other: | What are you talking about? I always let you talk. (denial) |
| You: | You think you always let me talk. (reflective response) |
| Other: | Yes, in fact I let you talk throughout the entire meeting today. |
| You: | Well, I don't like it when you begin speaking before I finish speaking, because I can't complete my thought. (restate message) |
| Other: | You're too sensitive. You should just talk over me! (diagnosing, diverting) |
| You: | You think I should just talk over you. (reflective response) |
| Other: | Yes, everyone has a lot to say, so just talk if you're worried about not getting enough air time. |
| You: | I can't complete my thought when you begin speaking before I finish speaking, and it frustrates me. (restate message) |
| Other: | So, you're bothered when I speak before you're finished. |
| You: | Yes. |

The chart on the facing page illustrates the relationship between feedback messages and active listening. As you can see, you may need to deliver your message, and respond with active listening several times before the tension level drops.

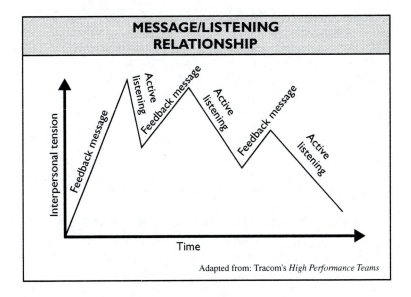

MESSAGE/LISTENING
RELATIONSHIP

Interpersonal tension

Feedback message

Active listening

Feedback message

Active listening

Active listening

Feedback message

Active listening

Time

Adapted from: Tracom's *High Performance Teams*

**Allow the other person to suggest a solution.**   You may already have in mind what you would like the other person to do to "fix" the situation. Even if you do, however, give him a chance to offer a solution first. When the other person comes up with a solution, he will often feel better about the idea and be more likely to implement it. At the same time, make sure the solution meets your needs also. Restate the solution for clarification and thank him. You might also agree to follow up later to talk about how it is working.

**Know you have done your part.**   You can't force someone to change his behavior. However, by delivering feedback thoughtfully and carefully, you can motivate someone to change behavior without creating undue tension and defensiveness. Since you can only control your own behavior, you have done your part responsibly and fairly.

## III.  RECEIVING FEEDBACK CONSTRUCTIVELY

Your own willingness and ability to receive feedback is also important to developing and maintaining positive one-to-one relationships.
Improving yourself professionally depends on receiving feedback
from your boss, peers, and employees—and altering your behavior
accordingly. In addition, by listening to someone's feedback, you
demonstrate concern for the other person, and you show that you
value his feedback by altering your behavior: both of these responses
will improve your relationships. First, consider how valuable feedback is for increasing your own self-awareness. Second, use the following guidelines to receive feedback constructively.

### 1.  Consider how feedback increases self-awareness.

Receiving feedback from others about your own behavior is one of
the most useful ways to increase your own self-awareness. A framework called the "Johari Window," developed by Joseph Luft (Jo) and
Harrington Ingham (Hari), illustrates the concept of different areas of
self-awareness. Among other things, the framework refers to the
extent to which you share and desire to share the knowledge, beliefs,
feelings, and behaviors that form your personality. The window has
four contiguous panes: one clear glass (the Open Self), one opaque
(the Unknown Self), one mirrored on the inside (the Blind Self), and
one mirrored on the outside (the Hidden Self).

| FEEDBACK AND SELF-AWARENESS | | |
|---|---|---|
| | **Known to you** | **Unknown to you** |
| **Known to others** | **OPEN SELF** | **BLIND SELF** |
| **Unknown to others** | **HIDDEN SELF** | **UNKNOWN SELF** |

SOURCE: J. Luft and H. Ingham

**Open Self:** The Open Self is shown as a clear glass windowpane, indicating your knowledge, beliefs, feelings, and behaviors that are known to you and known to others. As an example, you might be a morning person and be tremendously efficient and productive at that time. If everyone knows this about you, it is part of your Open Self. The more you share about yourself with others and consider others' feedback to you, the larger the Open Self becomes. The Open Self represents information about you that everyone shares.

**Hidden Self:** The Hidden Self represents aspects of yourself that you know, but others don't. Therefore, the Hidden Self is represented as a one-way mirror: clear glass to you, but mirrored to others so they can't see through. For example, perhaps your heart pounds whenever you are about to make a presentation. You are distracted and overwhelmed by this, but others can't see your pounding heart. Your anxiety at the beginning of a presentation is unknown to them, so they will not consider it when dealing with you. If they try to talk to you right before you deliver a presentation and you are too distracted by your pounding heart to respond, they may attribute your behavior to something else. While there are some things you may choose never to tell others, there are other things that might be helpful for others to know about you.

**Blind Self:** The Blind Self represents traits or behaviors that others know about you, but of which you are unaware. The Blind Self is represented as a one-way mirror which is clear glass to others, but mirrored to you so you can't see through.

There are several ways to minimize the size of the Blind Self and increase self-awareness. For example, seeing yourself on video-tape may show you some elements of your interpersonal communication of which you may be unaware until you see them on the video. We can also gain information about ourselves through assessment tools and inventories. More often, however, we gain insight into our Blind Self from feedback from others: acting upon feedback from others enables us to change and improve our behavior.

**Unknown Self:** The Unknown Self refers to aspects of yourself of which neither you nor others are aware. Therefore, the Unknown Self is shown as opaque to both you and others. An example of the Unknown Self might be how you would perform in a new and unexplored situation, such as how you might perform in a different job or career. It also refers to unconscious or subconscious patterns of behavior that might be explored in psychotherapy.

As you share information about yourself, and hear feedback from others, you reduce the sizes of the Blind Self, Hidden Self, and Unknown Self and increase the size of the Open Self: this framework encourages increasing self-awareness by hearing feedback from others and building trust and credibility by sharing with others.

## 2. Follow tips for receiving feedback.

Receiving feedback can be challenging and sometimes unpleasant. Think of times you have received feedback—such as in performance appraisals or in conversations with a boss, co-worker, or friend. Sometimes the sense that you're being assessed, even when receiving positive and supportive feedback, can be unpleasant. In preparation for receiving feedback then, consider the following tips.

**Breathe.**   Hearing feedback often creates tension. Many people hold their breath or feel their heart rate accelerate. Remind yourself to breathe deeply and try to feel your breath flowing into the bottom of your lungs. This will give you a moment to calm and collect yourself.

**Listen carefully.**   Try to listen for the overall sense of the feedback. Also, remember that not everyone who gives you feedback will be aware of the importance of objective, nonjudgmental descriptions of behavior and the impact of loaded words—so don't allow yourself to be derailed by challenging language. You can't control what the other person is saying, but you can manage your own response by practicing active listening techniques (attending, following, and reflecting).

**Ask questions for clarification.**   Avoid the possible inclination to argue; instead, ask questions to determine more specifically the nature of the feedback. While you are asking, remember to breathe and speak calmly.

**Acknowledge the feedback.** Paraphrase the feedback you have been given to acknowledge you have understood it. If the feedback was delivered poorly, full of criticisms or loaded language, try to paraphrase for clarification by choosing different language. For example, if someone said, "I was dying because you looked like a nervous wreck when you first started speaking in the meeting," you might paraphrase by saying, "You thought I looked uncomfortable when I first started speaking." This paraphrasing diffuses the judgment in the feedback and shows that you understood. Ask for specific examples and details to make the feedback easier to act on.

**Recognize valid points.** By recognizing the other person's valid points, you demonstrate that you value and respect that person's perspective. If you disagree with some of the feedback, you will have a better chance of being heard if you acknowledge points you agree with first.

**Don't react immediately; take time to sort out what you heard.** Avoid unchecked, visceral responses. Think about the feedback you have been given. If it's comfortable for you, discuss the feedback with a friend or someone you trust. Think about what you can do to address the feedback and change any behavior that can be changed.

---

In summary, developing feedback skills will improve your interpersonal and management effectiveness. Learn how to deliver and receive feedback effectively by practicing three-part messages to deliver both positive and negative feedback, and by combining active listening with the delivery of feedback. This will increase the chances that your feedback will be heard and that you will maintain positive and productive relationships. In addition, work to increase your own self-awareness by respectfully acknowledging and receiving feedback from others.

# CHAPTER III OUTLINE

I. Asking effective questions
   1. Using open questions
   2. Using other kinds of questions
   3. Avoiding challenging questions
II. Responding to questions
   1. Constructing responses with the questioner in mind
   2. Responding to difficult questions

# CHAPTER III

# *Questioning and Responding*

E ffective questioning and responding techniques are just as important to successful interpersonal interactions as effective listening and feedback. Instead of just letting the interrelationship of listening, questioning, and speaking happen—without plan or thought— (1) use questioning techniques to either elicit specific information or to develop a comfortable exchange, and (2) consider ways to respond to different styles of questions you may face.

# I. ASKING EFFECTIVE QUESTIONS

Understanding the differences between various types of questions will help you to identify situations in which to use them because the questions you ask will affect the information you gather. The questions you ask will also affect your relationship with the other person. Knowing the effect that different kinds of questions will have in an interaction will help you to ask the right questions for the right purposes.

## 1. Using open questions

If you have ever witnessed a courtroom drama, you have undoubtedly heard an attorney use open questions such as "Tell us in your own words . . . " followed by "And then what happened?" These classic "open questions" encourage the witness to focus on the details he considers important and to describe events naturally and comfortably.

Open questions encourage the other person to share information in his own way: they introduce broad topics and allow the other person to control the content and direction of his response. As a general principle, open questions are preferable in situations in which (1) building the relationship is important—since they invite the other person to express herself naturally and comfortably, and (2) understanding the other person's perspective and priorities is important—since they allow the other person to control the order and content of his response.

**Construct open questions.**   The key to asking open questions is recognizing that you are inviting the other person to control the content of her response. Your question may narrow a topic or provide direction, but it should allow the person free rein to concentrate on the material most important or memorable to her, and to develop her comments in her own style. Open questions generally begin in one of two ways.

- *With "How," "What," or "Why":* Questions that begin with these three words allow the other person to respond in his own way. For example, "How did you finally complete the project?" or "What are your concerns about your performance in this area?" or "Why are you interested in working here?"

- *By inviting details:* For example, " Describe for me . . . ," "Give me an example of . . . ," or "Tell me about . . . " are examples of ways in which you might invite detail by using open questions.

**Recognize the benefits of open questions.** Using these kinds of open questions has many benefits for the questioner and the person being questioned.

- *Benefits for the questioner:* Open questions are excellent for gathering information about someone's feelings and concerns. Open questions also allow you to discover the other person's priorities by giving him control of the content of his responses. Probing with open questions enables you to gather information from the perspective of the other person, which can be useful in tailoring responses, future questions, plans, assignments, or proposals for him.

- *Benefits for the person being questioned:* Most people enjoy responding to open questions since they control the content of their responses. These responses are comfortable and natural, especially when the questions are asked in a nonconfrontational manner and when the questioner listens effectively.

## 2. Using other kinds of questions

In contrast to open questions, other kinds of questions allow you to gather information in a more specific, directed way.

**Closed questions:**  Closed questions are important tools for isolating specific information and discovering facts and details. Closed questions do not invite open discussion, but instead limit and control the other person's response. Closed questions are useful when you are (1) dealing with an overly talkative person; (2) looking for a commitment, (such as "Can you stay for a 6:00 meeting?"); (3) refreshing your memory about a previously discussed issue, (such as "You got your MBA from Wharton, right?); or (4) establishing an absolute point of agreement or disagreement.

- *Structure questions for specific responses:* Examples of closed questions are: "Did you finish the project yet?" or "Are you happy with your performance in this area?" or "Will you be interested in working here?" These closed questions limit the speaker to a narrow range of responses.

- *By inviting specific details:* Know whether you want a "yes" or "no," or an exact date or time, and frame your question to invite only the response you want.

**Hypothetical questions:**  A hypothetical question often begins with "if" or "assume," and helps to gather information about someone's thought process or state of mind. For example, hypothetical questions might be useful in interviews if you want to ask someone about a possible management scenario, as in "Assume you are the manager of our information technology department. How would you recommend we handle rapidly changing technological options?" They might also be useful in exploring someone's comfort level with a new skill in a coaching situation, as in "Assume I told you to prepare for a negotiation with our office equipment vendor. How would you approach the task?" Don't use hypothetical questions to embarrass someone by exposing her inability to consider all aspects of an imaginary scenario, but do use them to understand priorities or breadth of thought.

**Forced-choice question:** "What's more important: having the signs printed on time or having them printed accurately?" is an example of a forced choice question which compels the respondent to choose options that are not necessarily mutually exclusive. These types of questions, like other closed questions, can be helpful in determining a specific answer, such as the ordering of priorities. They can be useful in a negotiation when you would like to limit the other person to only one of two options.

## 3. Avoiding challenging questions

Unlike the questions discussed previously, avoid the following challenging questions that may intimidate the other person and make productive responses less likely. Listen to your questioning style: if you tend to ask questions like these, consider what effect they are having on your interactions and relationships.

**Multiquestions:**   A multiquestion is a list of questions linked together. "Who said they were unwilling to meet with the client at 11:00 tomorrow, and why did they think we were planning a meeting at that time, and where should we hold the meeting, and what is the most important thing we have to let the client know at the meeting?" You can imagine the challenge the recipient of these questions would face: "Where do I start?" Therefore, before asking such an extended set of questions, pause for a moment, and consider breaking up the information you are looking for and dividing it into discrete questions.

**Loaded or leading questions:**   Loaded questions contain harsh or inflammatory language that may unflatteringly characterize someone's behavior or motives: "Do you always try to avoid work and pawn it off on someone else?" rather than "Do you usually distribute work around the department?" Leading questions assume the very facts you are asking about: "When did you stop stealing office supplies?" rather than "Have you ever taken any office supplies?" Instead of asking such questions, consider the impact negative language and characterizations will have on your relationship with the other person and choose more diplomatic wording.

**Rambling questions:**   Rambling questions are stream-of-consciousness expressions that lack direction or focus. A paraphrase can become a rambling question as you attempt to reflect back a speaker's comments for clarification. If your questions are unfocused, unorganized, or difficult to comprehend, pause and try to focus before continuing.

## II.  RESPONDING TO QUESTIONS

In business interactions like interviews, negotiations, and coaching sessions, you need to respond to questions asked by the other person in addition to asking questions. Give thought to your habits and patterns of responding.

### 1. Constructing responses with the questioner in mind

When answering questions, structure responses with the questioner in mind.

**Begin with an overview.**   Giving an overview of what you intend to say alerts the questioner to what she can expect you to cover in your response and signals the direction you want to take. The overview may take the form of a paraphrase of the question or a restatement of the concerns expressed. In addition, if you are unhappy with the language the questioner used to describe the topic of discussion, you can use the overview to reframe it. For example, in response to the question "What do you like about this proposal?", you might begin your response with the overview, "Well, there are two things I especially like about this proposal and one that concerns me."

**Provide details and examples.**   Many people tend to remember specific facts, statistics, anecdotes, quotes, and other details more readily than general concepts or issues. Including details and examples will make your comments more interesting and memorable. An anecdote describing how you managed a difficult employee is far more likely to be persuasive and memorable than simply saying you work well with others. If you are responding to questions about an increase in sales, for example, quantify the increase and the time frame, tell a story, or share a comment from your satisfied boss; don't just answer that sales have increased.

**Consider your language.**   Build rapport by using language and references the questioner will understand and appreciate, and avoid jargon and abbreviations that might alienate the questioner. To make difficult concepts friendly and accessible, use language that will be familiar to the listener. For example, don't overuse American sports analogies with an international colleague.

**Be aware of the questioner's behavior.**   Nonverbal behaviors such as strong eye contact, smiles, nods, or sympathetic expressions signal that she is interested in your comments and that you should continue to speak. On the other hand, if she is looking away, fidgeting, or toe-tapping she may be tired of listening. In such cases, you can (1) shift gears by asking an open question to invite her to redirect the conversation, (2) ask whether or not more details or examples are of interest, or (3) politely ask if your response is along the lines of what she is looking for or if other information would be helpful.

**Signal the conclusion of your response.**   Signal the conclusion with a summary like: "So that's a bit about my work history," or "So that gives you an idea of the steps we follow to ensure the accuracy of the information." Pause and wait to see whether the listener asks a follow-up question or for more detail; or you may check in by saying something like: "Does that answer your question?"

## 2. Responding to difficult questions

Although difficult questions often inhibit productive interactions, you may have to respond to such questions on occasion. If you are asked difficult questions like the ones described below, don't simply accept the set-up of the difficult question; rather, calmly and politely paraphrase the question to recast it in a less challenging light. Follow these tips for dealing with specific types of difficult questions.

**Multiquestions:**   If you are faced with a multiquestion, exercise good listening skills and begin with a paraphrase: "You have several questions about our upcoming client meeting. Let me see if I can answer your questions one by one," or group the questions in your mind and offer information: "You have questions about the plans for this meeting. Let me tell you what I know." If asked a multiquestion like: "Tell me why you went from Company A to Company B, and how that fit in with your interest in your current field, and why you want to work at this organization," you can begin your response with "Yes, let me tell you about my background and how it fits with my interest in this firm."

**Loaded or leading questions:**   Avoid repeating negative words and characterizations. For example, don't say "I don't always try to avoid work and try to pawn it off on someone else"; that response underscores the questioner's negative assessment of your behavior. Rather, acknowledge the other person's feelings or reactions in your paraphrase, but reframe the question: "You're concerned about the way I handled this job. I had another commitment last night and Lenny and Carl offered to finish the final steps." If asked a loaded or leading question such as "How long have you been ignoring these obvious problems?", you can begin your response by reframing the premise of the question: "Let me assure you of our dedication by reviewing the data collection and analysis process with you."

**Hypothetical questions:**   If you are asked a hypothetical question that makes you uncomfortable or puts you on the spot, frame your response in a way that notes the nature of the hypothetical. For example, if you are asked, "What would you do if you were in my shoes?", you might begin by noting that there are many aspects of the situation that you are not certain you have full knowledge of and you'd rather not speculate. Then, narrow the scope to that which you are comfortable answering: "I'm sure you have a variety of management challenges that may impact your control over the budget, however, if only looking at . . . ".

**Forced-choice questions:**   If you are asked a forced-choice question and are not comfortable making any of the choices offered, listen instead to the gist of the question. Reframe the question and address the broader issues it raises. For example, in response to "What do you value more, people or results?" you might begin by saying, "You're asking me about my management priorities . . . ". In addition, remember that you can answer either "both" or "neither" to a forced-choice question.

---

In conclusion, consider all the questioning options you have: keep in mind which kinds of questions are most useful for gathering specific information and which are most useful for building relationships. Avoid asking poorly phrased or inappropriate questions. In addition, learn to recognize difficult questions and practice strategies for responding to them.

# CHAPTER IV OUTLINE

I. Understanding social styles
  1. The "assertiveness" dimension
  2. The "emotionality" dimension
  3. The four social styles

II. Applying social styles
  1. Identify your social style
  2. Identify others' social styles
  3. Adapt your style to that of others
  4. Work effectively with others' styles

# CHAPTER IV

# *Social Styles*

People are different in many ways. Almost invariably, most people you interact with are quite different from you in terms of how they communicate, handle emotions, and deal with conflict and stress—as well as how they think, decide, listen, and talk. When you interact with someone who is different from you—and again, that is most people—it can be challenging to establish rapport or to be credible and persuasive. It can be even more challenging to create and maintain a positive and productive relationship.

The willingness and ability to appreciate and respond to various social styles is often what separates successful businesspeople from unsuccessful ones. What are social styles? Social styles are patterns of behavior in interpersonal interactions. Social style is not a description of personality, an indicator of ability or intelligence, or a predictor of success. However, social style *is* a strong predictor of future interpersonal behavior.

Understanding social styles can help you to understand what to expect in your interactions with others. Equally important, understanding the possible impact your own social style may have on others can help you to better manage relationships. Awareness of the social styles of others, along with the willingness and flexibility to make adjustments in your own behavior, can lead to more successful interpersonal interactions. This chapter describes the dimensions of behavior that determine social style, and the characteristics of the four social styles. In addition, it discusses how to apply social style information to improve and enhance business relationships.

## I. UNDERSTANDING SOCIAL STYLES

Social style is based on observable patterns of interpersonal behavior: verbal and vocal habits and patterns (what people say and how they say it), and nonverbal habits and patterns (what people do nonverbally).

**Your own social style:**   Reading about style differences can provide valuable insight into your own social style. However, the best way to explore the concepts of social style is to consider your own behavior by evaluating your own experiences: try to objectively make note of personal patterns, view yourself on videotape in social situations, and ask others for feedback.

**Others' social styles:**   To assess other people's social styles, note their patterns of behavior as objectively and nonjudgmentally as possible. Describing behaviors objectively and nonjudgmentally is challenging: try to avoid guessing at motivations for a person behaving a certain way, and just think of how to describe it objectively. For example, instead of "He's not happy unless he can stare me down, and rattle off the list of work he has for me," consider "He makes direct eye contact when speaking. He speaks more quickly than most people, and pauses infrequently." This approach will yield more useful information for assessing social style.

**A framework for viewing social style:**   An effective method for assessing social style, adapted from David W. Merrill and Roger H. Reid, is illustrated in the framework on the facing page. Before we discuss each of the four social styles, let's examine the two dimensions of behavior shown by the vertical and horizontal arrows below: (1) assertiveness (shown on the horizontal axis), ranging from "asking" to "telling," and (2) emotionality (shown on the vertical axis), ranging from "controlled" to "emotive." The following sections explain these dimensions.

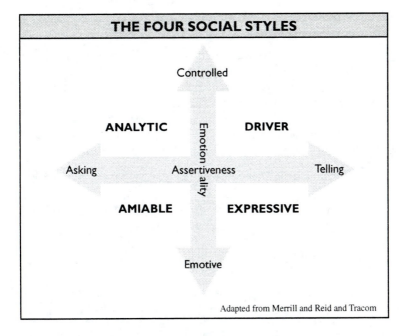

Adapted from Merrill and Reid and Tracom

## I. The "assertiveness" dimension

In social style, "assertiveness" (shown on the horizontal axis) refers to the perceived effort a person makes to influence others; the two ends of the assertiveness scale are "asking" and "telling." Your assertiveness style is determined according to where you fall along this continuum based on verbal patterns (word choice), vocal patterns (volume, rate, and length of pauses), and nonverbal patterns (posture, gestures, and eye contact). A person who falls on the "asking" side of the assertiveness scale is perceived to make less effort to influence others through verbal, vocal, and nonverbal behavior, whereas a person who falls on the "telling" side of the assertiveness scale is perceived to make more effort to influence others with those behaviors.

**Verbal patterns of assertiveness:**   Verbal patterns give clues to your assertiveness style.

- *Asking:* States opinions carefully; exerts little pressure for action; makes fewer and more indirect requests.
- *Telling:* States opinions strongly; exerts more pressure for action; makes more frequent and direct requests.

**Vocal patterns of assertiveness:**   Vocal patterns also provide clues about a person's social style.

- *Asking:* Usually speaks in softer voice; speaks more slowly; pauses frequently.
- *Telling:* Usually speaks in louder voice; speaks more quickly; pauses infrequently.

**Nonverbal patterns of assertiveness:**   Nonverbal behavior also provides clues to a person's social style.

- *Asking:* Leans back when speaking; makes intermittent eye contact when speaking; gestures less frequently and uses slower, smoother gestures.
- *Telling:* Leans forward when speaking; makes sustained eye contact when speaking; gestures more frequently and uses faster, more forceful gestures.

## 2. The "emotionality" dimension

Next, consider the emotionality scale—the vertical axis on the framework shown on the previous page. "Emotionality" is a measure of the degree to which a person's behaviors are perceived as emotionally controlled or emotionally expressive. The two ends of the emotionality scale are called "controlled" and "emotive." A person who falls on the "controlled" side of this scale is more guarded in emotional expression, while a person who falls on the "emotive" side of this scale will noticeably display his own emotions and react to the emotions of others.

**Verbal patterns of responsiveness:**   The kind of information someone includes in conversation gives clues to that person's emotionality style.

- *Controlled:* Prefers facts and details; limits talk of feelings; limits small talk.
- *Emotive:* Prefers stories, jokes, and anecdotes; engages in more small talk; shares feelings.

**Vocal patterns of responsiveness:**   Vocal patterns also give clues to emotionality style.

- *Controlled:* Speaks with limited vocal inflection.
- *Emotive:* Speaks with much vocal inflection.

**Nonverbal patterns of responsiveness:**   Nonverbal patterns of behavior also give clues to emotionality style.

- *Controlled:* Shows little facial expression; makes infrequent eye contact as a listener; gestures infrequently and uses many "palms down" gestures.
- *Emotive:* Shows much facial expression: smiles, nods, and frowns; makes frequent eye contact as a listener; gestures frequently and uses many "palms up" gestures.

### 3. The four social styles

By figuring where someone falls on the assertiveness and the emotionality dimensions, you can see which of the four social styles describes that person (shown in the four quadrants of the model): Driver, Expressive, Amiable, and Analytic. Each social style is generally associated with a cluster of interpersonal preferences.

**Drivers:**   Drivers combine "telling" assertiveness with "controlled" emotionality.

- *Behavioral patterns:* Speaks more quickly and loudly; speaks with little vocal inflection and infrequent pauses; maintains a rigid posture, possibly leans forward when interacting; gestures forcefully and makes sustained eye contact; states opinions directly; pushes for action; limits small talk or talk of feelings.

- *Characteristics:* Objective, determined, independent, pragmatic, efficient, and decisive

- *Orientation:* Action

- *Need:* To get results

- *Possible reaction to conflict:* Becomes autocratic.

**Expressives:**   Expressives combine "telling" assertiveness with "emotive" emotionality.

- *Behavioral patterns:* Speaks more quickly and loudly; speaks with varied vocal inflection; pauses infrequently; maintains a more relaxed posture; uses faster, more forceful gestures; uses much facial expression; shares feelings and engages in small talk.

- *Characteristics:* Imaginative, stimulating, enthusiastic, fun-loving, and spontaneous

- *Orientation:* Intuiting or relying on hunches

- *Need:* Social recognition

- *Possible reaction to conflict:* Verbally attacks

**Amiables:**    Amiables combine "asking" assertiveness and "emotive" emotionality.

- *Behavioral patterns:* Speaks more slowly and softly; speaks with varied inflection; pauses more frequently; maintains a more relaxed posture, possibly leaning back; uses slower, smoother gestures; uses much facial expression; shares feelings and engages in small talk.

- *Characteristics:* Friendly, dependable, easygoing, cooperative, supportive, and loyal

- *Orientation:* Feeling

- *Need:* To maintain relationships

- *Possible reaction to conflict:* Acquiesces

**Analytics:**    Analytics combine "asking" assertiveness and "controlled" emotionality.

- *Behavioral patterns:* Speaks more slowly and softly; speaks with little vocal inflection; pauses frequently; maintains a rigid posture; uses fewer gestures; uses little facial expression; limits small talk and talk of feelings.

- *Characteristics:* Industrious, systematic, persistent, detail-oriented, serious, exacting, and precise

- *Orientation:* Thinking

- *Need:* To be right

- *Possible reaction to conflict:* Avoids

## II. APPLYING SOCIAL STYLES

Social style is useful both for recognizing similarities and differences among people and for offering practical ideas about managing the differences. To apply social style information to interpersonal interactions, follow the steps described in this section: (1) know your social style, (2) know others' social styles, (3) adapt your style to others' styles, and (4) work effectively with others' styles.

### 1. Identify your social style.

Your habits and patterns of behavior shape others' perceptions of you. Regardless of whether these perceptions match your own self-perception, these habits and patterns of behavior—what others hear you say and see you do—are what they use to make determinations about you.

**Consider how others see you.**   Getting a sense of how others see you can be difficult, since how we see ourselves often differs from how others see us. Typically, others do not know much about your inner thoughts and feelings, but only know you by your statements and actions that they witness. For example, let's say you consider yourself serious and thoughtful at work; you write memos and review documents with intensity. You view yourself largely through this lens. When others appear, however, you put aside your work and always smile and chat, share personal information, and ask about their weekends and their families. Others will typically consider you to be friendly, warm, and talkative, since that is the behavior they see most often: it is part of your "social style." While others might know you work intensely, they will be more aware of your friendly, talkative self since that is how you behave when you are with them. Therefore, your self-perception of serious, thoughtful intensity—even if it reflects a great deal of your at-work behavior—may differ from the perception others have of you.

**Recognize your dominant style.**   You have a comfort zone of behavior that represents your dominant social style. It is no better or worse than any other style: it simply represents the pattern of your most comfortable behavior. In extreme circumstances, you may act outside of this comfort zone, but your dominant style will remain consistent. Obviously, there is much more to you than this style can describe—your dreams, values, goals, idiosyncrasies—yet it does describe your pattern of social behavior. You are similar to others with this style, although far from identical. Accepting that you have a dominant style, and that others also have dominant styles, will enable an understanding of social styles to work for you.

Once you have identified your own social style, through objective self-assessment and by considering feedback from others, it is time to consider the styles of others.

## 2. Identify others' social styles.

To determine someone else's social style, observe that person in a variety of daily situations. This way, you can detect prevailing patterns of behavior in a range of circumstances and not rely on unusual situations that may evoke uncharacteristic behavior. For example, how someone behaves when the company's stock has leaped 25 points or after being fired would fall outside typical daily patterns of behavior.

You can be most successful in determining the social style of someone you have known for awhile, have spoken with one-on-one, and have seen interact with others. Note typical patterns of behavior when that person seems most comfortable. Once you have determined your social style and the style of another person, you can then consider whether your styles are identical, compatible, or incompatible.

**Identical styles:**    You will probably feel most comfortable with someone whose style is identical to your own. For example, two Drivers will demonstrate similar verbal, vocal, and nonverbal patterns. They will find one another to be objective, efficient, and decisive, and appreciate each other's direct, action-oriented approach.

Similarly, two Amiables will feel comfortable with one another because of their similar verbal, vocal, and nonverbal patterns. They will find one another to be friendly, cooperative, and supportive and appreciate each other's efforts in building the relationship. The same feelings of similarity would be experienced by two Expressives together, or two Analytics together.

**Compatible styles:**    Compatible styles are alike along one dimension of behavior. The four compatible style pairings are:

- *Amiables and Expressives*, since both styles fall on the "emotive" side of the emotionality scale. Amiables and Expressives use much vocal inflection and facial expression; they will gesture frequently with "palms up" gestures; they will make frequent eye contact as listeners; they want to build relationships by sharing stories, jokes, and feelings. At the same time, Amiables and Expressives are dissimilar along the assertiveness scale: they will sense their differences in vocal volume and pace; amount and intensity of eye contact when speaking; speed and forcefulness of gestures; and forcefulness with which they make requests.

- *Analytics and Amiables* both fall on the "asking" side of the assertiveness scale. Analytics and Amiables will speak more slowly, softly, and less forcefully in making requests and expressing opinions; they will gesture more slowly and make less eye contact as speakers; they will feel comfortable with one another's cautious, nonconfrontational patterns. At the same time, they will sense their differences along the emotionality dimension: the Amiable will speak with vocal inflection and facial expression and use "palms up" gestures, and will want to engage in small talk and share anecdotes, jokes, and feelings. The Analytic will limit vocal inflection and facial expression, use "palms down" gestures, and prefer to focus on facts and details.

- *Analytics and Drivers* both fall on the "controlled" side of the emotionality scale. Analytics and Drivers will limit vocal inflection and facial expression; use "palms down" gestures; limit small talk and talk of feelings; and focus on facts and details. Analytics and Drivers will sense their differences along the assertiveness dimension: they will sense differences in vocal volume and pace, in the amount of intensity of eye contact and gestures, and the forcefulness with which they make requests.

- *Drivers and Expressives* both fall on the "telling" side of assertiveness. Drivers and Expressives will speak quickly, loudly, and more forcefully in making requests and expressing opinions; gesture frequently with faster, forceful gestures; lean forward and make sustained eye contact when speaking. They will feel comfortable with one another's direct, assertive style. The Driver and Expressive will sense their differences along the emotionality dimension: the Expressive will want to engage in small talk and share anecdotes, jokes, and feelings, and use much vocal and facial expression; and the Driver will limit vocal and facial expression and prefer to focus on facts and details.

**Incompatible styles:**     Incompatible styles are shown in the quadrants diagonally opposite one another; they are not alike along either continuum of behavior. Typically, interpersonal situations between individuals with incompatible styles are the most challenging. These two incompatible style pairings are:

- *Driver and Amiable:* As they interact, the Driver and Amiable will sense their dissimilarity in vocal and nonverbal patterns, as well as in verbal exchanges. They will probably feel interpersonal tension. The Driver will push for action and results, which will frustrate the Amiable's attempt at building a relationship. The Amiable will want to make a personal connection by engaging in small talk and story-telling, which will frustrate the Driver's interest in results. If the frustration leads to conflict, the Driver will become autocratic—in an attempt to achieve action—and the Amiable will acquiesce—in an attempt to maintain the relationship.

• *Analytic and Expressive:* Consider an interaction between an Expressive and an Analytic. The Expressive values opinions and hunches, and is comfortable making quick guesses and discussing possibilities. Alternatively, the Analytic likes to gather data and consider them carefully. He wants to make a thoughtful and correct decision and is uncomfortable jumping to quick conclusions. You can see that the orientations of these two opposing styles would lead to challenges in the interaction. As they interact, the Analytic and Expressive will sense their dissimilarity in vocal and nonverbal patterns, as well as verbal exchanges, and they will probably feel interpersonal tension. The Analytic will want to collect and thoughtfully evaluate information so he can make a right judgment or decision. The Expressive will want to intuit information and make quick decisions and discuss future possibilities. If the frustration leads to conflict, the Expressive will increase attempts at interaction and possibly verbally challenge the Analytic—and the Analytic will avoid.

## 3. Adapt your style to that of others.

You can facilitate interactions by modifying your behavioral patterns to adapt to the other person's style.

**Accommodate the other's needs:**   Express yourself along the other person's wavelength, without abandoning your own naturalness.

For example, an Expressive could accommodate the needs of an Analytic by slowing her pace, talking less, listening more, providing and considering more factual information. Alternatively, an Analytic could facilitate an interaction with an Expressive by quickening his pace, talking and interacting more, and considering opinions and hunches as valuable information.

**Mirror others' nonverbal behaviors.**   Even more specifically, consider vocal or nonverbal patterns. The gestures of an Analytic might be described as smaller and infrequent. The gesturing patterns of an Expressive might be described as more frequent, faster, and forceful. Therefore, an Expressive who is approaching an interaction with an Analytic might consider controlling and limiting her gestures during the interaction. Mirroring the gesturing patterns of the other person will reduce tension in the interaction by demonstrating "likeness" between the two.

**Move toward your opposite style.**   To be even more effective at dealing with others, consider moving toward your areas of discomfort by adopting some of the behaviors of your incompatible style. For example:

- *Analytics*, whose orientation is to think, can grow by moving toward the Expressive orientation, and declaring or expressing their thoughts.
- *Drivers*, whose orientation is to act, can grow by moving toward the Amiable orientation and listening to others to build and maintain relationships.
- *Expressives*, whose orientation is to spontaneously intuit or rely on hunches, can grow by moving toward the Analytic orientation and analyzing and checking assumptions.
- *Amiables*, whose orientation is to build and maintain relationships, can grow by moving toward the Driver orientation and initiating activity.

## 4. Work effectively with others' styles.

Recognizing and responding to different styles will earn you the endorsement of others who will find you to be tactful and reasonable. If you respond only to your own comfort and needs, others will find you difficult, inflexible, and argumentative.

**Practicing versatility:** By being aware of and adapting your behavior to others' social styles, you can facilitate more comfortable interactions. For example, when working with:

- *Drivers:* Ask questions about specifics and stick to "what" questions. Don't waste time trying to build the relationship, but get right to the task at hand. When discussing issues, support the position, not the person. Be specific on areas of disagreement: remember that Drivers want to move into action quickly, and getting them to slow down and listen to others will be a challenge.

- *Expressives:* Discuss future goals and possibilities, and not present realities and details. Explore mutually stimulating ideas and look for areas of agreement. Avoid arguing: Expressives like to win competitive verbal exchanges. Take the initiative in handling details. Be cautious in planning: expressives sometimes enthusiastically accept more than they can handle.

- *Amiables:* Demonstrate an interest in the person. Establish a cooperative environment and communicate patiently: draw out personal opinions. If agreement is easily reached, gently and nonconfrontationally explore areas of possible future disagreement. Express gratitude for the Amiable's contribution.

- *Analytics:* Demonstrate through action, not words. Do not overstate or oversell; stick with facts and logical, proven conclusions. Take time to remain persistent and don't expect quick implementation. Praise the Analytic's strategy and planning.

**Help others:** You can improve interactions with others by helping them to perform in ways that challenge them. For example:

- *Amiables resist initiating activity.* Facilitate the Amiable's growth action by encouraging her to initiate activity in supportive and encouraging ways. An Amiable will not initiate if she feels she will bother or anger someone else, but will initiate if she feels she is being of helpful service.

- *Analytics resist declaring their thoughts.* Facilitate the Analytic's growth by encouraging him to declare hunches and by not highlighting or criticizing when hunches are not right.
- *Drivers resist slowing down to listen to others.* Encourage Drivers to slow down and listen by highlighting how listening to others improves results.
- *Expressives resist checking facts and assumptions.* Facilitate the Expressive's growth by encouraging her to check facts and assumptions and pointing out how she will be recognized for careful, thorough work.

---

In summary, you can enhance and improve interpersonal relationships through awareness of social or behavioral styles—your own and others'. You will work then more effectively with others and be able to adapt your style when appropriate. Versatility will enable you to improve your business interactions and relationships.

# PART II

# *Application Opportunities*

After you have practiced and improved your abilities with the building block skills described in Part I, you will approach opportunities to apply and integrate these skills with greater confidence. The application opportunities addressed in Part II require you to move quickly between listening, delivering feedback, asking and responding to questions, and demonstrating an awareness of social styles. These common application opportunities are:

- **Chapter V:** How do you plan for and perform in an interview?
- **Chapter VI:** How do you plan for and perform while conducting a performance appraisal or similar coaching opportunity?
- **Chapter VII:** How do you plan for and perform in a negotiation?

In addition to reviewing the building block skills from Part I, this section offers guidelines for planning for these specific interactions and offers suggestions on how to structure and behave during the interactions.

# CHAPTER V OUTLINE

I. Interviewing a candidate
   1. Prepare for the interview
   2. Conduct the interview
   3. Assess the candidate and the interaction

II. Being interviewed
   1. Before the interview
   2. During the interview
   3. After the interview

# CHAPTER V

# *Interviewing*

An interview can be a powerful and often stressful interpersonal experience—whether you are conducting the interview or being interviewed. Interviews are as different and varied as the combination of any two people can be, so all interviews contain elements of surprise. However, preparing well for an interview can reduce the number of surprises and ensure that important messages are delivered.

This chapter focuses on job interviews, but many of the principles relating to interview preparation and process apply to other interview situations—such as information gathering for careers, projects, or reports—as well. This chapter first addresses the interviewer's perspective: how you can (1) prepare for the interview, (2) conduct the interview, and (3) assess the candidate and the interaction. Second, this chapter addresses the experience of the interviewee: what you should do (1) before the interview, (2) during the interview, and (3) after the interview is over.

## I. INTERVIEWING A CANDIDATE

You may be like many professionals who feel they are too busy to put much time into preparing for an interview. You might take a quick glance at a résumé two minutes before the candidate walks in the door. However, if you don't plan any specific questions to direct the interview toward your own interests and objectives, you will probably end up with just a vague sense of what the candidate is like and with whatever details he chooses to share.

Planning ahead, however, for even just a few minutes, can be beneficial in two ways. First, by establishing your objectives for the interview, you increase your chances of selecting the best candidate for the position, not simply the person you came out of the interview process liking or remembering the most. Second, you will save time: good interview planning and techniques will lead to your choosing a better candidate, which in turn will mean you will be far less likely to have to interview for that candidate's replacement soon.

### 1. Prepare for the interview.

As an interviewer, you probably have two different general objectives for any interview: to sell the candidate on your organization and to assess the candidate. Make these objectives as specific as possible before you begin.

**Develop your sell strategy.**   Write down your sales objectives in advance:

- *What you want the candidate to know:* What do you want the candidate to know about your organization as a result of the interview? You may have several points in mind. For example, an objective of yours might be something like: "As a result of this interview, the candidate will know the following three things about our expectations for the department's future." Think about when and how during the interview you intend to convey this information.

- *What you want the candidate to think:* For example, if one of your objectives is to give the candidate a positive impression of the office environment and staff, consider how you will accomplish that objective during the interview. Where will you conduct the interview? Who else might the candidate meet? What literature or materials might you share with the candidate? Remember your behavior will influence his impression of your organization as well.

**Develop your assessment strategy.** Also, think in advance about how you will assess the candidate.

- *Establish your interview objectives.* Design your objectives to reflect your interests as specifically as possible. For example, if you want to assess team experience, you might have the following objective: "As a result of this interview, the candidate will share at least three examples of relevant team management experience." Perhaps you want to assess problem-solving ability: "As a result of this interview, the candidate will guide me through the process she uses to solve several different management problems." Then plan your questions to achieve your interview objectives. What will you ask to encourage the candidate to share such information? If the candidate is unable to provide you with satisfactory examples, you can consider that to be valuable information as well.

- *Review the interview form or job description.* Often large organizations have standard forms available to evaluate interview candidates. If you are using such a form, be sure it matches the skills and traits of the job for which you are hiring. Think about the day-to-day environment and consider what other skills or traits might be crucial but might not have made it to the standard form or job description. If you are not working with an interview form or job description, you should think specifically about skills and traits you would like to assess and create your own record-keeping document for the candidates you will interview.

- *Identify the skills and traits you are looking for.* First identify the skills you would consider prerequisites for the job, and skills which could be learned on the job through training or coaching. In addition to skills, think about character traits or preferences. For example, having an interest in detailed work might be a trait you would want to identify in the interview. Traits are often difficult to detect in a screening interview, but posing forced-choice questions can be a start. For example, "Would you rather analyze a balance sheet or deliver a presentation on the results of the analysis?" If you are clear about the nature of the work, many people will discover a mismatch between their preferences and a job themselves.

- *Focus in depth on critical skills and traits.* Limit the scope of what you are trying to accomplish during the interview so you have time to go beyond the first response for information. Probe in depth to determine the extent of a candidate's skill level in a critical area. For example, present a hypothetical scenario and ask the candidate to describe how he might approach the problem.

- *Coordinate with other interviewers.* If the candidate is interviewing with more than one person at your organization, take the time to meet in advance with the other interviewers to discuss an interview plan. Make sure you agree upon which traits are important to assess, and then consider dividing the responsibility of probing in depth for a particular trait among the different interviewers.

**Develop questions.**  Draft some questions you will use to gather information from the candidate. As described on pages 36–37, use open questions to encourage discussion and closed questions to nail down facts. If you would like the candidate to provide examples and anecdotes to describe her skills and traits, begin questions with phrases like: "Describe for me," "Explain how," "Tell me about," "Detail or highlight for me," or "Give me an example of," which encourage the other person to speak. If you need to verify a fact, ask closed questions beginning with "Did you," "Have you," "When," or other phrases that lead the candidate to respond yes or no, or with brief and specific detail. In addition, if you don't know already, check with your human resources department to clarify which questions are legal and which are not.

**Think about your interviewing style.**  Depending on your preferred interviewing style, you may find the following tips on questioning and record-keeping useful.

- *Structured approach:* This approach is characterized by developing checklists, noting each response, asking consistent questions of each candidate, and planning the timing of each interview segment. If you have a structured style, or plan to use such an approach for a particular interview, you may want to use some of the following questioning techniques to build conversation and get more in-depth responses from candidates.

  *1. Follow up with probing questions.* Use probing questions to make the interview more conversational, such as "What was the most challenging thing about that situation?"

  *2. Ask for additional examples.* After the candidate offers an example of a skill or trait, ask for one or two additional examples to investigate the depth of her knowledge or experience.

3. *Use negative balance questions.* Ask the candidate to provide a contrasting example to a positive story, such as "You seem to be good at leading groups. Was there ever a time you weren't able to pull a group's factions together, and how did you handle it?"

4. *Use reflective statements.* Paraphrase the candidate's comments and wait for her to respond: "So, you never have an issue with deadlines?"

- *Free-form approach:* This approach is characterized by spontaneous, conversational questioning. If you have a free-form approach, or plan to use such an approach for a particular interview, it may require you to focus on time control and evaluation techniques. Too much conversation can lead you away from your interview objectives.

  1. *Establish talking points to stay on track.* Decide what points you want to cover ahead of time and write it on your assessment form.

  2. *Create an agenda.* Create an agenda for yourself with approximate timing and stick to it. Perhaps sharing the agenda with the candidate will help keep you aware of your time commitment. Place a clock in a spot where you can glance at it without seeming rude. If you need help, ask a colleague to pop in at a certain time to remind you to move forward with the interview.

  3. *Be silent and let the candidate talk.* Don't fill too much time with your own comments. Silence is an effective probing technique, too. Let the candidate talk.

**Consider alternative interviewing techniques.** Instead of asking standard interview questions, consider the following alternative techniques.

- *Reaction to the workplace:* Take the candidate around the workplace and ask for her reaction to the environment, pace, or culture.

- *Job performance:* Ask her to perform some aspect of the job: an accountant might analyze a balance sheet, a secretary might type a letter, a salesperson might deliver a brief presentation.

- *Personality interview:* Ask questions that probe judgment or maturity, or give you a sense of her values and choices. For example, "How do you define success?" or "What three words would others use to describe you?"

- *Past performance interview:* Base questions on the candidate's past, asking for specific examples to support skills and traits you are seeking, such as "Give me an example from your work at Howard & Fine that demonstrates your team leadership abilities."

**Develop a record-keeping grid.**   Since many personal qualities blend together, you may lose track of which ones you are aiming to identify during the interview. To help yourself stay on track, write the key skills and traits you are looking for in a candidate across the top of a sheet of paper. Use this to make notes of examples and anecdotes the interviewer shares to describe his abilities in these areas. The following grid shows an example of a record-keeping document to use for an interview.

| SAMPLE RECORD-KEEPING GRID | | | |
|---|---|---|---|
| **SKILLS AND TRAITS** | Leading a team | Negotiating contracts | Making presentations | Evaluating proposals |
| **EXAMPLES** | | | | |
| | | | | |
| | | | | |
| | | | | |

SOURCE: L. Russell, Professional Development Company

## 2. Conduct the interview.

Choose an interview environment and set the tone in a way that will put the candidate at ease so you can get the best information for your purposes.

**Choose an appropriate environment.** Choose a comfortable location, free of distractions and interruptions.

- *Make arrangements in your office.* If you will be interviewing in your office, consider whether your sitting behind your desk is appropriate or if having chairs around a smaller table or other arrangement might be more suitable. Generally, being seated behind your desk will set a more formal and authoritative tone while being seated at a small table or on comfortable office furniture will set a less formal and friendlier tone.

- *Make arrangements elsewhere.* Perhaps you intend to conduct interviews in a conference or meeting room. If so, make sure the room is available and suitably prepared. Decide if part of the interview will include a visit to a different location, like a shipping department or factory floor, and coordinate the arrangements.

- *Plan hospitality arrangements.* If you intend to offer the candidate coffee or a soft drink, plan for it. Check in with other people you would like the candidate to meet. Coordinate restaurant reservations ahead of time.

**Set the tone.**   A strong, friendly handshake will help set a positive tone. Make a pleasant comment on a general topic. If you would like to be on a first-name basis with the interviewer, be sure to let him know.

**Preview.**   After the initial small talk is over, let the candidate know how long the interview will last and how you intend to use your time together. Let her know what general areas you would like to cover, if she will be speaking with other people, or when she should ask any questions she might have.

**Use explicit transitions.**   Let the candidate know when you are finished discussing his résumé and would now like to move into some case scenarios, or when you are ready to respond to any questions he might have, or when you only have a few minutes left.

**Let the candidate talk.**    Be sure to give the candidate enough air time. In an assessment interview, follow the 80/20 rule and allow the candidate 80 percent of the time to speak. In a "sell" interview where you are providing information for the candidate's consideration, you may be talking more than 20 percent of the time.

**Close.**    Tell the candidate about next steps. Then be sure to follow up when and how you said you would.

### 3. Assess the candidate and the interaction.

When the interview is over, it's time to assess the candidate by reviewing the following components of the interview.

**Consider skills and traits.**    Remember to assess the skills and traits you identified and not to rely solely on your gut reaction. Although your feelings about someone are important, they are hard to assess and document. Note your feelings about the candidate, but also return to your interview objectives and assess the candidate's key skills and traits by filling in the record-keeping grid described on page 68.

**Go beyond first impressions.**    Your first impression of the candidate might have been so powerful it influenced other perceptions. Could a strong start have caused you to miss reasons to reject the candidate? If a nervous candidate calmed down halfway through the interview, should you overlook a weak opening? Consider the first impression as you write your evaluation of the candidate. In addition, be aware of your own knee-jerk biases. For example, is the candidate a graduate of your alma mater—or of a rival college?

**Consider your own effect.**    How did you contribute to the personality mix? Were you the reason the candidate was so nervous? Was your style so different it took you a long time to build rapport?

**Be specific, descriptive, and legal.**   Make sure your written assessment is a useful document to you and others who might need to use it as part of an evaluation of a candidate. Ask your human resources department to determine corporate policies on recording and releasing interview evaluations. In general, using descriptive accounts of behavior is more helpful that using judgmental terms. For example, it's generally safer to document "candidate did not provide specific example of leadership when asked" instead of "candidate is not a leader." Examples and details are useful in backing your assessment, but only document information according to the practices of your company. In addition, using a standard process ensures that each candidate has an equal chance.

**Assess yourself.**   Find the time to do some self-assessment. By monitoring your progress interview by interview, you'll gradually be able to improve your own interviewing skills. Did you achieve your interview objectives? Did you create a comfortable environment and put the candidate at ease? Did you follow the 80/20 rule? Did you allow the candidate to finish her answers? Think about how you can perform even better in the future.

## II. BEING INTERVIEWED

When you are on the other side of the table being interviewed, consider your goals and objectives from a different perspective. Preparing well for an interview will not only make it more likely you will get a job, but it will also give you a stronger basis to make your job selection. Be prepared for the impromptu speaking nature of the interview: you can't control what questions will be asked of you, but you can control your answers.

### I. Before the interview

Prepare for the interview by gathering information about the company for which you are interviewing. Review the cover letter and résumé you sent that got you the interview and make sure you have the appropriate interview attire. In addition, prepare for the actual interaction in the following ways.

**Analyze the audience.**   Conduct a thorough audience analysis. Review the job description. If you can, find out as much as possible about the person(s) who will be interviewing you. Then, as precisely as possible, determine the skills and traits the company is looking for in a candidate. Go beyond "interview-speak" characteristics such as "strong analytical skills" or "excellent communication skills." Figure out exactly what type of analytical skills are essential to the job: what kinds of documents and details would you need to review, what type of analysis would be required, or what types of reports would be produced? In terms of communication skills, are they looking for someone who is good at management activities that require strong interpersonal skills, conducting meetings, writing reports or letters, or designing and delivering presentations? Ideally, you should develop a short list of several skills or traits that correspond to what the company thinks is most important for you to have for the job.

**Define your interview objective(s).**   As specifically as you can, determine your interview objective(s), such as, "As a result of this interview, the interviewer will hear that I have strong planning and negotiating skills and that I am practiced at analyzing financial data."

**Construct an anecdote grid.**    Arm yourself with anecdotes about and examples of your experience and skills; connect them to your interview objective(s). These anecdotes will demonstrate that you are a qualified candidate for the job by linking desirable skills and traits to examples from past jobs or other experiences. Examples and anecdotes will be far more memorable to the interviewer than vague generalities or broad claims. To develop these anecdotes, create an anecdote grid along the lines of the following example.

| SAMPLE ANECDOTE GRID | | | |
|---|---|---|---|
| | Leading a team | Negotiating contracts | Making presentations | Evaluating proposals |
| Current job | XYZ project | ABC vendor fiasco | XYZ presentation | • Training options • Computer leases |
| Past job | Department spin-off | Renewing office lease | Weekly status meetings | |
| Graduate School | Finance project | | • Student leadership • Marketing final | |
| Volunteer | Park clean-up | Soliciting donations and price reductions | | Event venues |

SOURCE: L. Russell, Professional Development Company

- *Write key skills and traits across the top of the grid.* Use the job description or other information you have gathered about key skills or traits needed to do the job to write headings across the top of the grid.
- *Write main headings from your résumé down the side of the grid.* Your current job, previous jobs, graduate work, college, significant hobbies, interests, or anything that represents a major heading on your résumé belongs here. Write these down the left side of the grid.
- *Complete the grid with anecdotes.* Take some time to remember experiences you had at your jobs and in school and try to come up with examples that complete the grid. Try to have an anecdote or two for

just about every box on the grid. For some boxes, you will have many anecdotes. For example, if presentation skills appears at the top of your grid, you might note examples such as specific presentations from your current job, your past job, as a college student, or as a volunteer. You might also note any presentation skills training and courses you have attended.

**Rehearse from your grid.**   Using the notes from your anecdote grid, test out your best examples by telling the stories aloud. If you had the opportunity to talk about your most recent negotiation experience, for example, what would you say? Consider your best examples based on what you know about the company, the job, and the interviewer. Imagine how the interviewer would react to different details and wordings. By rehearsing from your anecdote grid, you prepare yourself for the interview and, perhaps more importantly, you design your material for the interviewer.

- *Follow the one-minute rule.* Try to make each example a minute or less in the telling. Consider what you will add if you are given a nonverbal signal to continue or if you are asked a follow-up question.

- *Include only relevant details.* Avoid boring stories, and don't go off on unrelated tangents. Always remember your objective in telling the story. Know the conclusion you want the interviewer to draw about you and keep details relevant.

- *Don't memorize.* Rehearse, but don't memorize. Keep your style conversational.

**Plan answers to questions.**   Think about some of the classic interview questions, such as: "What is your greatest strength?" "What is your greatest weakness?" or "Where do you see yourself in five years?" Be truthful yet thoughtful in your responses. For example, your greatest weakness may be something obvious from your résumé, such as the fact that you lack international work experience or have not managed more than ten people. Using it in your example allows you to diffuse the interviewer's possible concerns and mention how you are addressing the weakness. In addition, consider how you will respond effectively and politely to any of the difficult questions outlined on pages 42–43.

**Plan your opening remarks.** Most interviewers begin with small talk and a preview of the interview. Soon after, however, interviewers often "kick off" with a standard open-ended question such as "Tell me about yourself" or "Walk me through your résumé." This is an invitation for a self-structured introduction that should be brief, interesting, and forward-thinking.

- *Brief:* At this point, the interviewer does not want to know that you switched high schools in your sophomore year, or that you traveled to Australia last December, so don't attempt to describe everything on your résumé in this one response. Give the interviewer enough information to start a conversation, but not too much, so you tax her listening skills. Don't speak for more than about a minute.

- *Interesting:* A detail or two may be more interesting than generalizations. Note that touching on information of interest to the interviewer requires good audience analysis: what does she most want to know about you?

- *Forward-thinking:* Your opening comments should somehow relate to why you are interviewing for this position. Make your opening remarks forward-thinking by connecting your background to your interest in the job. Try to link your skills to benefits for the interviewer or company.

**Plan to respond to the interviewer's style.** Review the social styles material on pages 46–59, and consider how someone with each of the four different social styles might behave at the start of an interview. For example:

- *Driver:* A Driver might give a solid handshake, make direct eye contact, sit erect or lean forward, speak forcefully with limited vocal inflection or facial expression, and move directly into the interview.

- *Expressive:* An Expressive might also give a solid handshake, make direct eye contact, sit casually, and speak forcefully with much vocal inflection and facial expression. An Expressive might begin with small talk and storytelling.

- *Amiable:* An Amiable might give a gentler handshake, make direct eye contact as a listener but less eye contact as a speaker. An Amiable might lean back when speaking, and speak more softly but with much vocal inflection and facial expression. An Amiable might begin with some friendly questions, small talk, and storytelling.

- *Analytic*: An Analytic might give a gentler handshake, make infrequent eye contact, and sit erect. An Analytic might speak more softly with little vocal inflection or facial expression, and might limit small talk to move directly into the interview.

Consider how you might alter your behavior depending on the interviewer's social style.

**Plan your appearance.**   First impressions count for a lot. Plan to dress in a way that communicates your understanding of the job. To make that decision, imagine the interviewer wants to hire you on the spot, but needs the immediate approval of the CEO: would what you are wearing communicate that you are the right person to hire? With that in mind, dress appropriately and comfortably.

## 2. During the interview

Arrive a few minutes early for the interview and make sure you are comfortable: hang up your coat, have a drink of water, gather your thoughts. If you are feeling a little anxious, calm yourself by taking a few long, slow deep breaths. During the actual interview, pay attention to the following components of interpersonal interactions.

**Recall the power of first impressions.** A firm handshake, direct eye contact, and a smile when you first meet someone are important in Western business culture. Since interviews often start with casual small talk, be ready to make a pleasant comment about your trip getting there, the waiting area, or the interviewer's office. Try not to let any manifestations of nervousness derail you from moving through the initial, sometimes anxious, moments.

**Respond to the interviewer's style.**    As you meet the interviewer, consider her style. Don't try to be someone you are not, but adjust your style to be companionable and comfortable with the interviewer.

- *Social style:* Is she leaning back in her chair, smiling broadly, gesturing smoothly and showing you pictures of her children and pets? Or is she leaning forward with a serious expression, speaking precisely and getting right to business? You can help make the interaction comfortable by responding in kind to her style: if she would like to engage in small talk, listen, ask questions, and share appropriate information. If she would like to get right to business, don't force small talk, but move directly into the interview.

- *Level of detail:* In addition, take note of the level of detail and the kind of information that might be most valued by the interviewer. Does he seem more interested in facts and results or casual talk and anecdotes?

**Use effective listening and speaking nonverbals.**

- *Use an involved posture.* Sit with the small of your back against the back of the chair and your feet flat on the floor. Cross your legs if they are hidden under the table or desk in front of you. Place your hands loosely on your lap and gesture comfortably when you are speaking—but, show your respect and interest as a listener by not fidgeting.

- *Make eye contact.* Look at the interviewer when she is speaking. Look at the interviewer while you are speaking. It's fine to look away while

you are thinking, but you should be making eye contact about 75 percent of the time.

- *Don't interrupt.* Allow the interviewer to finish asking the entire question before you begin answering. In addition, respond politely to difficult questions such as those outlined on pages 42–43.

**Use examples from the anecdote grid.**   Whenever you have the
opportunity in the interview, share an anecdote that reinforces one of
the key skills and traits the job requires. Using examples from the
anecdote grid (described on page 73) will more effectively prove
your abilities than simply asserting you have the skills the interviewer is looking for. Remember that stories with concrete details
will be more memorable than general claims. Finally, if you are
asked a broad question like: "How did you enjoy graduate school?"
you can respond by including an anecdote or two that illustrates your
key skills and traits and helps you to achieve your interview objectives.

**Structure comments.**   For long answers, structure your responses
with the listener in mind. Begin with a preview or overview statement, follow with details or examples, and then summarize the main
messages. Don't be too heavy-handed about this: there will be many
conversational moments that won't need these kinds of structured
responses.

**Include closing remarks.**   Think about whether you've delivered
your intended message. Perhaps you can work in another example to
reinforce either your key skills or your interest in the company. Or
perhaps you want to close simply by expressing enthusiasm for the
job. The closing is memorable. It can't always overcome a poor first
impression, but it can reinforce a strong performance. Always
remember to thank the interviewer for her time.

## 3. After the interview

An employer's interview process may take several weeks or months. Your follow-up may make the difference between you being remembered or forgotten.

**Send a thank-you note.** Distinguish yourself from other candidates by sending a thank-you note or letter. Try to send the note within one day of the interview while the meeting is still fresh in both your and the interviewer's mind. In your correspondence, refer to something from the interview that reinforces your interest in the job. Link your background and experience to job requirements whenever possible so the interviewer remembers how he will benefit from hiring you. Consider the style of the organization and the interviewer in deciding if a typed, handwritten, or emailed thank you is appropriate.

**Assess your own performance.** Review the interview and evaluate the interaction and your responses. Did you meet your interview objectives by getting your key messages across? Was your appearance and behavior appropriate and comfortable? While the experience is fresh in your mind, make notes to yourself about things you did well, as well as things you would do differently next time.

---

In summary, good interviews take some preparation and rehearsal. If you are interviewing someone, you should establish interview objectives and prepare questions or comments that help you to achieve those objectives. Use a planning or record-keeping grid to ensure that you have considered and remembered all the important information. In addition, think about the types of questions that will yield the best results for your purposes. If you are preparing to be interviewed, rehearse, but don't memorize, your opening comments and key anecdotes. Behave as comfortably, naturally, and politely as you can during the interview as you attend to the other person's style. Finally, follow up by assessing the interaction and your contribution, to improve your interviewing technique for the future.

# CHAPTER VI OUTLINE

I. Negotiation strategy
   1. Consider the context of the negotiation
   2. Establish your interests
   3. Analyze the other person's context for the negotiation
   4. Use persuasive techniques

II. Listening and questioning
   1. Use effective listening techniques
   2. Gather information with effective questioning

# CHAPTER VI

# *Negotiating*

We all negotiate every day in small ways. Allocating resources within your department, enforcing policies and procedures, establishing agreements with vendors or subcontractors—or even deciding which movie to see with a friend—are all examples of routine negotiations. Although you may prepare extensively for complex negotiations involving high stakes, you may not give much thought to everyday negotiations. However, even preparing briefly for a simple negotiation can yield great benefits. This chapter explains how to (1) determine your negotiation strategy and (2) use effective listening and questioning techniques during a negotiation.

# I. NEGOTIATION STRATEGY

Think about three elements to determine your strategy for any negotiation: (1) the context of the negotiation, (2) your own interests, and (3) the other person's perspective.

## 1. Consider the context of the negotiation.

First, consider the context of the negotiation. The context is determined by your relationship to the other person, the importance of the outcome of the negotiation to you, and your typical approach to conflict.

**Your relationship to the other person:**   Consider your relationship to the other person, and evaluate the importance of that relationship to you.

- *Important relationship:* If, for example, you are negotiating with a valued colleague or boss, you might consider the relationship to be extremely important. Your strategy will need to reflect your interest in preserving and possibly even improving the relationship. In situations like these, you might choose to reject options that could make the other person feel like a "loser," and decide to collaborate or accommodate.

- *Less important relationship:* On the other hand, if you are negotiating with a difficult vendor who could easily be replaced, or with an unreasonable employee, you might choose to achieve whatever you can—with little concern about preserving the relationship—and compete. In other situations you might decide that the relationship is either so soured or unimportant that the effort is not worth it and plan to avoid the negotiation altogether.

**Importance of the outcome:**   In addition to considering your relationship with the other person, evaluate how important the outcome of the negotiation is to you.

- *Important outcome:* If the outcome of the negotiation is very important to you, you will want to collaborate or compete to maximize what you can achieve.

- *Less important outcome:* If the outcome is less important, you may decide to accommodate the other person's needs in light of the bigger picture, or even to avoid the negotiation completely and let the chips fall where they may.

After considering the importance of your relationship to the other person and the importance of the outcome to you, decide which of the following strategies makes sense for you to apply in the negotiation:

## CONTEXT OF NEGOTIATIONS

|  | | Substantive outcome important? | |
| --- | --- | --- | --- |
|  | | Yes | No |
| **Relationship important?** | Yes | **COLLABORATE** | **ACCOMMODATE** |
|  | No | **COMPETE** | **AVOID** |

SOURCE: Adapted from G. T. Savage, J. D. Blair, and R. J. Sorenson

- *Collaborating:* Collaborative negotiations typically require the most thought and preparation. Collaboration is common in long-term relationships and aims for a "win-win" solution. Sharing backgrounds, reasons, and concerns may allow for undiscovered solutions to benefit both parties.

- *Competing:* Competitive negotiations—considered to be "win-lose"—are more common in one-time interactions such as haggling over the price of a car or settling a lawsuit.

- *Accommodating:* You many choose to accommodate the other person's interests when the relationship is important and the outcome or the negotiation is less important to you. This "lose-win" option also makes sense if you want to create goodwill in hopes of achieving what you want in a future, more important, negotiation.

- *Avoiding:* If neither your relationship to the other person nor the outcome of the negotiation is important to you, you may choose not to invest any time and avoid the negotiation completely.

Because it may be difficult to clearly assess the importance of the relationship or outcome, you may find that many negotiations will not fall squarely into one of the four strategies represented in this framework. However, you may be able to reject at least one or two possible options, such as, "There is no reason for me accommodate or avoid in this negotiation, so I should think along the lines of competing or collaborating."

**Your approach to conflict:**   Do you generally tend to welcome most interactions—however difficult—or do they make you feel tense? Are you comfortable with challenges and disagreement or does the disapproval of another person disturb you? Do you like to compete or do you prefer to avoid?

- *What is your interpersonal style?* Consider your approach to interpersonal conflict by assessing yourself on the assertiveness scale on page 47. If you are on the "asking" side of the assertiveness scale, you may prefer to avoid or acquiesce (accommodate) as tension increases. If you are on the "telling" side of the assertiveness scale, you may become autocratic or verbally attack the other person as tension increases. Keep in mind your interpersonal tendency and decide if you can work with it, or if you will need to work against it, in a particular negotiation.

- *What if your style and strategy are inconsistent?* If there is an inconsistency between your interpersonal style and the appropriate strategy you identified in negotiation framework, consider rehearsal and training to prepare yourself for the negotiation. For example, if you tend to be averse to competing and the situation calls for it, you might benefit from staging a role-play with a friend or colleague to help you construct your approach. A role-play may also help you to practice how you will manage your feelings and behavior during the negotiation.

## 2. Establish your interests.

After considering the context of the negotiation, think about the following aspects of the negotiation.

**Assess your objectives.**    Outline the topics of negotiation as you see them so you have a big-picture view of everything that might be considered. Try to prioritize your objectives for each of those topics. Then, as specifically as possible, establish a "Like," "Expect," and "Must" position for each negotiation point. By doing so, you will become aware of possible trade-offs you may be willing to make in terms of the complete negotiation.

- *"Like":* What is the best or ideal outcome for you?
- *"Expect":* Given the other person's objectives, what is the likely and acceptable outcome for this point?
- *"Must":* What is your true bottom line for this point? Establishing this bottom line can sometimes be a challenge; however, identifying it removes the anxiety of making on-the-spot concessions that may undercut your best interests.

**Determine your BATNA:**    Your BATNA is your "Best Alternative to a Negotiated Agreement." In other words, if you are unable to negotiate an agreement with the other person, what will you do? Investigating and developing your BATNA will strengthen your negotiating position. For example, if you are renegotiating your office lease, you might decide your BATNA is to move to new offices. If so, find out as much as you can about real alternative locations, and even think through the logistics of moving. Having a realistic view of your BATNA will enable you to better perform in the negotiation.

**Rehearse aloud.**    After you have established a "Like," "Expect," and "Must" position for each point, try to articulate aloud why they are important to you, so you will feel more prepared to do so in the negotiation. Stating reasons aloud like this sometimes reveals that certain thoughts or ideas don't make sense or are inappropriate to share with the other person. Always figure out in advance why you hold a certain point of view. If you can't do that—for example, because you don't want to reveal sensitive or confidential information—practice saying aloud that you cannot share it and explain why you cannot. Practice until you are able to articulate your ideas and reasons clearly and calmly. Since having a strong BATNA increases your negotiating power and having a weak BATNA diminishes it, consider how you will either share or shield your BATNA during the interaction.

**Consider the larger picture.**   How far-reaching is the impact of this negotiation?

- *Consider other people.* Do you need to consider other people who might be affected by the negotiation? For example, if you are negotiating a salary increase for one of your employees, consider the impact that giving a large raise to her might have on other people in the department if (and when) the word gets out.

- *Consider other issues.* Will the outcome of this negotiation affect a tangential issue? For example, if you successfully negotiate a long-term lease in a new building, how will your boss react to being fifteen miles farther from his health club?

- *Consider outside-the-box issues.* Clarify the limits of the negotiation. You may be worrying unnecessarily about an unrelated point. Or you may be ignoring a connection to a larger issue—like how the outcome of this negotiation will affect an upcoming negotiation with another colleague—and want to rethink your approach.

**Reframe the negotiation.**   Consider reframing the points you have established by deciding if you can position some in a different way.

- *Use a point to establish a precedent.* For example, can the timing of a particular event be considered not as an independent fact, but as representative of how other events will be planned? If this sales meeting must fall on the first Tuesday of the month, then can we plan that all sales meetings will fall on the first Tuesday of each month?

- *Move something outside the specific negotiation.* For example, if you can agree to seven of eight points, can you move forward with those seven and table the eighth point for a later date?

## 3. Analyze the other person's context
## for the negotiation.

Put yourself into the shoes of the other person and try to figure out how he will be approaching the negotiation.

**Consider the other person's negotiation context.**    If possible, don't rely only on your own assumptions about the other person, but get insights from others who know him.

- *Importance of the relationship:* Do you think he considers your relationship important? If so, he may plan to collaborate or accommodate. If not, he may plan to compete or avoid.

- *Importance of the outcome:* Do you think a substantive outcome for this negotiation is important to him? If so, he may plan to collaborate or compete. If not, he may plan to accommodate or avoid.

- *Approach to conflict:* Assess his assertiveness style. How might you expect him to behave in the negotiation? Also, talk to someone with a similar style and get a read on how that person might order or arrange an approach and process.

**Assess the other person's objectives.**    Write down what you consider his "Like," "Expect," and "Must" positions as described on page 85 for each of the points of the negotiation.

**Determine the other person's BATNA.**    The more you can learn about the other person's BATNA before and during the negotiation, the better able you will be to push or yield on certain points.

**Stage a role reversal.**    Especially in a high-stakes negotiation, you might benefit from a role-play in which you reverse roles and take the side of the other person. Forcing yourself to see things from the other person's point of view and arguing for his position can reveal hidden compatibilities between the two positions or clarify true points of tension. In addition, this type of role-reversal exercise can help you see the merits of the other person's position and make you more understanding of his point of view, so you can behave reasonably and calmly.

**Probe for information.**    During the negotiation, probing for information may lead you to reassess the other person's context, so be prepared to adjust your own approach.

## 4. Use persuasive techniques.

Your ability to achieve good results during a negotiation depends on many factors. Although some of these factors—like plane schedules or the timing of a holiday—may not be in your control, you may be able to influence others. Consider using elements of persuasion that can help the other person find hidden value in your proposals.

**Assess your credibility.**  What does the other person know about you in advance, or what will he learn about you in the negotiation? Your reputation and behavior will affect the interaction and possible outcome of the negotiation. Consider how to best communicate your most important credentials to the other person.

- *Credibility before the negotiation:* How well does the other person know you and what does she know about you? Does she know anything about your style? Might she know any details of your background that would influence her? For example, many people are influenced by someone's title, years of experience, education, or endorsement by a highly respected individual or institution. In addition, if you have the reputation of being fair, honest, and reliable, and if you behave that way in the negotiation, the other person will be comfortable accepting your description of events and details. If you have a reputation for being less than completely candid, and you reinforce that reputation through your behavior in the negotiation, the other person will probably feel cautious and want to check the accuracy of your statements. If you are representing someone else in this negotiation, be sure you have the authority to speak for that person and are able to communicate that authority with confidence.

- *Credibility during the negotiation:* What will make you appear credible to the other person? Decide whether you are looking to reinforce similarities or differences with that person. How would you like that other person to perceive you? According to Mary Munter, some ways to increase your credibility during the negotiation are: (1) *Rank:* Share your title or associate yourself with a high-ranking person. (2) *Goodwill:* Emphasize benefits to the other side. (3) *Trustworthiness:* Offer balanced views, and acknowledge any conflict of interest you might have. (4) *Expertise:* Associate yourself with or cite authoritative sources. (5) *Image:* Use nonverbals that will appeal to the other side, including dress and behavior. (6) *Common ground:* Uncover similarities in values, ideas, and background.

In addition, think of how you can further build your credibility through your behavior by appearing confident, competent, and comfortable.

**Use principles of influence.** Consider how you can incorporate the principles of influence studied and evaluated by Robert Cialdini.

- *Liking:* Generally, people prefer to agree—rather than disagree—with people they like, so increase the likelihood of agreement by being likeable: be friendly, empathetic, and interested in the other person. Look for comfortable opportunities to build bonds and lower defenses by exploring backgrounds and experiences and finding similarities in schools, hometowns, hobbies, interests, or opinions. Share sincere, positive remarks about the other person's behavior or attitude. Your interpersonal graciousness will establish trust and encourage the other person to give you the benefit of the doubt in case of a misunderstanding.

- *Reciprocation:* Most people tend to reciprocate courtesies, favors, and gifts. Extend a courtesy to spark a courtesy or instill goodwill. Plan to make a concession on a point that may mean little to you in hopes of igniting a reciprocal concession on a point that matters to you.

- *Commitment and consistency:* Once people commit aloud or in writing to a principle or statement, they tend to want to remain consistent with that commitment. Therefore, in a negotiation, ask for verbal or written acknowledgment of points of agreement, or have the other person agree with aspirational statements of resolution to reinforce cooperation, such as "We can work this out, right?"

- *Social proof:* People will tend to look for confirmation of ideas, beliefs, and actions from others, especially others who are similar to them: the notion that "other people are doing it" can be powerful. Have information about similar individuals or institutions to reinforce the notion of the socially accepted, correct or expected response.

- *Scarcity:* The less available something is, the more desirable it can appear. Limit the timing or availability of something and the other person may want it more, and want it now. For example, if supplies are diminishing, you might make a deal today.

- *Authority:* Your own expertise or your association with other credible sources may be important to the other person. Incorporate this information carefully to avoid bragging and name-dropping.

## II. LISTENING AND QUESTIONING

Once you have finished your planning and the negotiation has begun, consider how you can gather more information throughout the negotiation to further develop your strategy. Apply the techniques of effective listening and questioning from pages 3–16 and 36–39. Your ability to apply these fundamental skills is essential to success in negotiations.

### I. Use effective listening techniques.

Using effective listening during the negotiation will increase your chances of success. Effective listening does not mean abandoning your own position or faking agreement with the other person. Rather, effective listening has many benefits in the negotiation.

- *Gather information.* Listening to the other person will enable you to gather a lot of information about her person's priorities, feelings, frames of reference, and position simply by giving her room to talk.

- *Diffuse tension.* In addition to gaining understanding of the other's point of view and frame of mind, listening will diffuse unnecessary tension by giving her the satisfaction of being heard.

- *Enhance your credibility.* As a listener, you have the power to demonstrate reasonableness, consideration, and other qualities that contribute to your credibility. You will be more persuasive if you show that you have considered the other person's point of view by listening effectively.

**Use effective nonverbal behavior.**   Know your listening nonverbal habits and be thoughtful about using these signals in Western cultures.

- *Eye contact:* Make direct eye contact with the other person, even if you think you can listen effectively without it. Looking at the other person sends a signal to her that you are paying attention. Effective eye contact does not mean 100 percent eye contact. Look at the speaker about two-thirds or three-quarters of the time. In other cultures, different standards apply: in Asia, for example, direct eye contact can be viewed as a challenge or sign of aggression. Investigate cross-cultural nonverbal differences beforehand to reduce the possibility of inadvertently offending or alienating the other person.

- *Body position:* Face the other person squarely and lean in slightly. Avoid slouching, turning away, or placing feet on the table, which are signs of disrespect.

- *Facial expression and arm gestures:* Crossing your arms, bowing your head, and furrowing your brow can signal disagreement; alternatively, nodding your head, smiling briefly, and saying "uh-huh" will not only encourage the other to continue speaking, but might suggest agreement with her message.

- *Seating arrangements:* A negotiation where two people sit on opposite sides of a desk or table can feel competitive and adversarial; a negotiation where two people are side-by-side or are seated at a low, round table can feel more cooperative.

**Paraphrase the other person's comments.**   Paraphrasing, as discussed on pages 11–12, can lead to better understanding of the other person's views and often diffuses heated exchanges. In paraphrasing, look for opportunities to recap points you agree with and acknowledge the other person's efforts: for example, "That is an effective way of describing our disagreement," or "Your approach makes sense, and you've identified where our main differences lie." Incorporating acknowledgments of the other's efforts will promote a cooperative atmosphere. Try to avoid focusing only on points of disagreement, and include statements that point to areas of agreement, such as, "Looks like we're clear about how to resolve our differences in the Pittsburgh and Cleveland orders, so now we need to figure out a way to deal with Niagra Falls," rather than "We are in trouble with Niagra Falls."

**Avoid ineffective replies.**   The other person might behave unreasonably. Don't escalate exchanges in any of the following ways:

- *Don't return insults.*

  Other person: The options you are giving me are unbelievably limited!
  You: So you don't think you have many choices.
  NOT: Well, you haven't exactly given me a lot to work with!

- *Don't get personal.*

  Other person: This process is a disaster.
  You: You aren't happy with this process.
  NOT: You're a disaster!

- *Don't criticize.*
  Other person: Our phone conversation was worthless.
  You: You were frustrated by our conversation.
  NOT: If you had listened with more than half a brain we might have gotten somewhere.

**Ask the other person to paraphrase your comments.**   One way to diffuse a negative interaction or to lower someone's tension is to ask him to paraphrase your points back to you. By doing so, you can check that he understands your message and get him to acknowledge your points without battling against them.

**Use passive listening occasionally.**   In contrast to the kind of active listening described above, passive listening is useful when dealing with an overly talkative or emotional person. Sit quietly, but do not engage in any encouraging nonverbals. Wait for the other person to run out of steam.

## 2. Gather information with effective questioning.

Asking questions that encourage the other person to talk will help you to gather information.

**Ask noncombative questions.**   Ask noncombative and open questions that invite the other person to describe his thinking, or share his feelings and concerns, such as, "What ideas do you have about how to approach these issues?" Avoid asking questions that use inflammatory language or that serve no other purpose than for you to let off steam. Don't get sucked into tit-for-tat rhetorical battles or name-calling. Questions that will cause the other person to feel uncomfortable may derail the negotiation, such as, "How on earth can you say that?" or "Don't you think we've waited too long already?"

**Ask questions that elicit useful information.**

- *Open questions:* (who, what, when, where, why): "Why are you concerned about this timing?" "Who will be most affected by this and how will they be affected?"
- *Invitations to express thoughts and feelings:* "What are your thoughts on this issue?" "How do you feel about this proposal?"
- *Background questions:* "Can you tell me what happened next?" "How long ago did you get involved?"
- *Fact-finding questions:* "What price do you currently pay for these items?" "Where are the materials located now?"

**Avoid asking provocative questions.**

- *Loaded questions:* "Are you sitting there saying you're taking the lazy, thoughtless approach and you'll never budge on this point?"
- *Boxing- in questions:* "Don't you agree that this is the only reasonable solution?"
- *Unrelated questions:* "By the way, what do you think I should tell my staff about why this meeting is taking so long?"

**Respond carefully to provocative questions.**  Minimize the possible escalation of conflict by considering the following types of responses if the other person asks you a provocative question:

- *Are you saying you're taking the lazy, thoughtless approach and you'll never budge on this point?* "I'm saying that I feel certain I cannot accept less than I told you."
- *Don't you agree that this is the only reasonable solution?* "We need to explore every option."
- *By the way, what do you think I should tell my staff about why this meeting is taking so long?* "You'll need to decide what is appropriate to tell them."

**Remember to probe for information.**  In competitive negotiations—and sometimes in collaborative negotiations—a person will often bluff or conceal his bottom line. In addition, a negotiator might unintentionally not share certain information if he believes it to be irrelevant to the negotiation. Be prepared to ask probing questions to gather the information you need; you might uncover hidden compatibilities between interests. Follow up with questions to get at the underlying reasons for the other person's position.

---

In summary, prepare for any negotiation first by evaluating the context of the negotiation: consider the importance of your relationship to the other person, the importance of the outcome of the negotiation to you, as well as your preferred approach to conflict. List the points of the negotiation and establish your objectives for each of the points. Then analyze the other person's negotiation context and think through how you might influence the other person's decision-making. Finally, use effective listening and questioning techniques throughout the negotiation.

# CHAPTER VII OUTLINE

I. Developing coaching skills
   1. Consider the benefits and skills of coaching
   2. Design SMART objectives
   3. Attend to the employee's perspective

II. Structuring the session

# CHAPTER VII

# *Performance Appraisals*

Performance appraisals should be used as coaching opportunities whenever possible. In assessing an employee's work, consider the performance appraisal as a chance to support or improve performance, resolve problems, or teach skills and share knowledge. These types of coaching goals require extended and focused feedback from you to an employee, but can begin or be reinforced during a performance appraisal.

Like most communication activities, conducting performance appraisals and providing follow-up coaching takes time and energy. An effective organization will recognize your willingness and ability to develop your employees through these efforts. This chapter covers (1) the skills needed to effectively conduct performance appraisals and include elements of coaching, and (2) the structure of a performance appraisal session.

## I. DEVELOPING COACHING SKILLS

Most performance appraisals can be used as opportunities to coach as well as to evaluate. Usually, when people think of "coaching" they think of sports activities. In sports, a good coach is critical to the success of an individual player or a team. The advice, support, motivation, skill development, and training discipline that a coach provides can make the difference between a stagnant and a stellar performer. Coaches don't have to be the best at the skill they are teaching: in fact, we know that many coaches can't, and maybe never could, perform with the same skill and talent as the people they coach. However, good coaches do have to know how to instruct and inspire the people they coach.

The coach–athlete relationship may be helpful to consider as you begin to conduct employee performance appraisals. Try to imagine how an athletic coach might approach her interactions with her athletes: How might she communicate expectations for performance? How might she identify strengths and areas for improvement, and communicate what those areas are? What goals might she set and why? How might she inspire, motivate, and teach? How will she encourage, support, and criticize? In addition, think about the behaviors you have appreciated in the people who have taught and coached you throughout your life, and try to replicate the most positive and helpful of those behaviors.

## I. Consider the benefits and skills of coaching.

Coaching, like all effective management practices, has many benefits for you and your organization. To be effective, coaching requires a certain set of skills.

**Benefits of coaching:**

- *Benefits to the coach:* Coaching benefits you as a coach: you can (1) relieve yourself of routine tasks, (2) delegate tasks with greater confidence, (3) have time and peace of mind to focus on other challenges and grow professionally.

- *Benefits to the organization:* Coaching helps the organization to (1) understand the skills and talents of its employees, (2) improve employee productivity through careful and focused instruction, and (3) increase employee morale and self-confidence.

**Skills needed for coaching:**   Effective coaching requires a variety of skills for these benefits to occur.

- *Interpersonal skills:* The building block skills described in Part I of this book are important in coaching. (1) *Listening:* When asked to identify the qualities of the best coaches or teachers they have ever had, many people name the ability and willingness to listen above all others. By listening effectively, you will develop a trusting relationship; promote cooperation; and learn about the issues, concerns, goals, and hopes of the person you are coaching. (2) *Providing feedback:* By providing feedback effectively, you can increase someone's awareness of his strengths and abilities and provide specific recommendations for improvement. (3) *Questioning:* By using effective questioning techniques you will gather information that will help you to target your coaching endeavors. (4) *Social style awareness:* By considering the social style of the other person, you can facilitate better interactions and motivate your employees.

- *Organizational skills:* A coach needs organizational skills to schedule sessions, keep records, measure efforts and results, and follow up.

**Willingness to coach:**   In addition to these critical skills, effective coaches must also have a sincere willingness to coach. The best coaches get to know a lot about an employee; develop thoughtful, innovative ways to help him make improvements; and have helpful or caring attitudes.

## 2. Design SMART objectives.

After considering the benefits of incorporating coaching elements into your performance appraisals, and assessing your own skills and willingness to coach, you can start to prepare for the interaction. The topics addressed in a performance appraisal should be based on agreed-upon responsibilities and standards of behavior—from the employee's job description, for example. Employees should never be surprised in a performance appraisal to find that they are being evaluated in a never-before-discussed area. If developmental areas are identified in a performance appraisal, plan to establish a coaching or training schedule for the employee.

Begin by defining the scope of the relationship. As you approach each performance appraisal, keep in mind your goal to motivate that person to better performance, and your notion of what that better performance will look like. What aspects of someone's job performance are subject to your efforts? Clarifying the scope up front will help you focus on what feels comfortable and appropriate for the relationship, as well as what is important to the job.

Once the scope of the relationship is clear, decide upon objectives. In addition, make sure the objectives are focused on the employee rather than on you. In other words, the effectiveness of a coaching relationship or individual session is measured by the changes in the employee, rather than by your activities. Create objectives that meet the five criteria listed below:

---

### ESTABLISHING *SMART* COACHING OBJECTIVES

**S**trategically driven, and a **S**tretch
**M**easurable
**A**ttainable
**R**einforceable
**T**ime-bound

**Strategically driven and a Stretch for the employee:**
Strategically driven objectives are those that are tied to the goals and interests of the organization. The objective should also be challenging—or a Stretch—for the employee. Assigning a mundane task to someone does not require a coaching commitment, but developing a higher-level skill, like learning to manage a client relationship, might.

**Measurable:** Establish a baseline for someone's performance or knowledge so you can measure progress. This means quantifying your objectives whenever possible. Avoid broad, general goals such as "will be better" or "will show improvement." Change general objectives such as "improve budget estimating skills" to measurable objectives such as "improve budget estimating skills so third quarter estimate falls within 10 percent of third quarter actual." Identify exactly how improvement will be measured. For example, "Thirty percent of Larry's sales presentations between January and March will result in signed contracts with clients" would be a measurable objective.

**Attainable:** While objectives need to be a stretch for the employee, they can't be unattainable. Don't make objectives too easy, but remember that you can always set new ones as the coaching relationship progresses: consider reassessing and redefining objectives as necessary. In addition, achieving an objective is a great morale booster, so consider the motivational aspects of celebrating an accomplishment.

**Reinforceable:** Reinforce objectives through new opportunities. Allow the coachee to exercise new skills by integrating them into her responsibilities. For example, the objective "Thirty percent of Larry's sales presentations between January and March will result in signed contracts with clients" suggests that Larry's sales presentations will be more effective. Reinforce this objective by giving him the opportunity to deliver presentations and get feedback about them so his presentations can improve.

**Time-bound:** Agree upon a length of time to attain the specific, measurable objective. Having a "deadline" will help focus the employee's efforts. At the end of the agreed-upon time, meet again to clarify or rework any unmet objectives.

## 3. Attend to the employee's perspective.

Once you have established SMART objectives, consider the employee in anticipation of the interaction: (1) the employee's social style, (2) your credibility with the employee, and (3) the employee's learning preferences.

**The employee's social style:**   Using the information we discussed on pages 46–59, evaluate the employee's social style. What type of interpersonal behavior might you expect from the employee? For example, will she be inclined toward small talk and storytelling (Amiable or Expressive), or will she prefer to stick to business (Analytic or Driver)? In addition, what might she be most motivated by: achieving results (Driver), being right (Analytic), social recognition (Expressive), or building relationships (Amiable)? Consider how you might acknowledge the particular interest(s) of the employee and use it to motivate her during the session. In addition, consider whether her style is compatible or incompatible with your own style and anticipate how it might affect the interaction. For example, if you are an Amiable you might like to begin interactions by building a relationship with small talk. If you are coaching a Driver, she might prefer to get right to business and be frustrated by this type of opening to a session.

**Your credibility:**   How does the employee perceive you? Your credibility (described in more detail on pages 88–89) will affect your effectiveness. If the employee doesn't find you credible, you'll need to solve this problem before you begin coaching. For example, don't assume that you have credibility simply because you are her boss. Find out more about what aspects of your background she does value.

- *Your credentials:* Your status and title within your organization, as well as your education, affiliation with an institution, or relationship with a valued individual may all be important to the person you are coaching. Your experience and expertise in the area in which you are providing coaching will probably be important as well. Think about what he might know about you already and what additional information you might want to share with him.

- *Shared background and values:* Similarity in background and values between you and the employee may also enhance your credibility. For example, perhaps you attended college in the same state, or both support a similar social cause or charitable organization. Uncovering commonalities between the two of you can be important in establishing a trusting relationship.

- *Your interest in coaching the other person:* In addition, your credibility is likely to be affected by your perceived interest, and your willingness to help the employee. Prepare yourself to explain the benefits of what you are hoping to achieve for the employee. Think of how you might persuade her. Your goodwill in assisting with her skill development should enhance your credibility with her. Using good listening and feedback skills is a good way to show your interest.

**The employee's learning preferences:**  Another effective coaching tool to consider is the learning preferences concept described by Neurolinguistic Programming (NLP). NLP categorizes three individual preferences for learning and recalling information: visual, auditory, and kinesthetic. For example, when coaching meeting management skills, you might first approach the task in the following ways to accommodate three different learning preferences:

- *Visual preferences:* People with a visual learning preference respond well to visual representations of information such as models, and pictures or charts. For someone with a visual learning preference, you might begin by observing a videotaped example of someone leading a meeting, or by modeling meeting management yourself.

- *Auditory preference:* People with an auditory learning preference respond well to traditional classroom teaching methods like lectures and discussions. For someone with an auditory learning preference, you might begin by describing and then discussing principles or examples of effective meeting management.

- *Kinesthetic preference:* Kinesthetic learners learn best by doing and they like active or experiential learning. For someone with a kinesthetic preference, you might begin by allowing him to manage a meeting, and then reflect on the experience.

When coaching someone, think first about your own learning preference; you will probably first try to coach or teach to that preference. Then, think about the employee's learning preference. However, don't limit yourself to only approaching coaching one way for any one person: each of these different approaches might be helpful for someone with any preference at some point in the coaching process.

## II. STRUCTURING THE SESSION

This section details a six-step process for approaching an annual performance appraisal or coaching session.

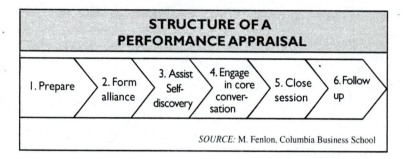

### STRUCTURE OF A PERFORMANCE APPRAISAL

1. Prepare 〉 2. Form alliance 〉 3. Assist Self-discovery 〉 4. Engage in core conversation 〉 5. Close session 〉 6. Follow up

*SOURCE:* M. Fenlon, Columbia Business School

**Step 1: Preparing:** Prepare by doing several things in advance of the actual performance appraisal or coaching session. As described earlier in this chapter:

- *Establish objectives.* Establish SMART objectives both for the coaching relationship and for each coaching session as described on pages 98–99. For example, the overall objective of the relationship may be to improve the employee's performance as a purchasing agent or to improve her ability in negotiating contracts. For a specific session, however, the objective may relate to one particular aspect of that skill. Either be able to express the objectives clearly yourself or develop them jointly with the employee.

- *Analyze social styles.* Consider the employee's social style and your own style as described on pages 46–59. How might you put her at ease? What might you anticipate in the interaction?

- *Analyze your credibility.* As described on pages 88–89, consider your credibility and how to enhance it.

- *Gather documentation.* In advance, gather any necessary documentation or records.

- *Role-play a difficult session.* In preparation for a difficult session you might want to role-play with a colleague.

- *Find a comfortable place to meet.* Ensure that the meeting environment is comfortable for both parties and suitable for listening and talking.

**Step 2: Forming an alliance:** "Forming an alliance" has to do with how you open the session, by establishing a positive rapport and tone.

- *Opening:* (1) You may want to consider the style of the other person to determine what might be most helpful in setting a positive tone and putting the other person at ease. For example, while some people find that engaging in small talk builds the relationship and contributes to credibility by promoting shared interests and values, others find small talk to be a frustrating time-waster and prefer to get right to business. (2) Some managers like to ask questions and explore the employee's goals before voicing their own ideas. Others like to find common interests that will make the transition to the coaching process more comfortable. (3) If credibility is an issue, you may need to spend some time discussing your experience or other helpful information.

- *Preview:* Once you have set the tone, bridge to a "preview" so the employee will understand how the session will be structured. The preview usually includes information about the meeting's content and the topics you hope to cover. Also address timing: how long the session will last and how much time will be devoted to each topic. In many cases, a flexible approach to timing is preferable, but a written agenda can be useful in formal situations.

**Step 3: Assisting with self-assessment:** Encourage the employee to "self-assess" so you can understand how her perceptions of her performance differ from or agree with your perceptions. One clear benefit of using self-assessment is that the process may increase the employee's sense of responsibility and ability to own up to her performance issues. People are often much harder on themselves than a coach would be, so you may have to help employees focus on their strengths.

- *Use listening skills.* At this stage, your listening and questioning skills are key. You should often engage the employee as a partner and solicit perceptions of his strengths or areas for improvement. Use open questions to help gauge the employee's mood and focus. Making records of someone's knowledge, skill, and feelings at the beginning of a coaching relationship is often helpful. You can use these records as a benchmark for comparison as coaching efforts progress. Follow the guidelines for effective listening from pages 3–17.

- *Share your assessment.* Here is where you can share your assessment of the employee's performance. Be sure you have notes and documents to support your assessments. Ask the employee for comments. Don't surprise the employee by assessing performance in areas not previously discussed. Follow guidelines for effective feedback from pages 19–29.

- *Reinforce good performance.* Praise the employee on areas of strong or satisfactory performance. Let her hear your appreciation of the high standards of her work in certain areas. Later in the session, you can reference these high standards as representative of the work she can aspire to in other areas.

- *Deal with discrepancies.* When there are discrepancies in perceptions, you need to clarify and address these areas. Clearly, conflicts in perceptions and opinions need to be openly discussed. They can be leveraged as valuable opportunities for learning and information exchange.

- *Use self-disclosure.* During this stage, you may also decide to engage in some self-disclosure and share information or experiences related to the issues discussed to build "goodwill" credibility. Remember that the session needs to be about the employee; do not divert the focus of the meeting by rehashing too many of your own "war stories."

**Step 4: Engaging in the core conversation:**   During the "core conversation" you narrow the session's focus.

- *Focus on a specific area.* The core conversation should be about concrete and specific performance issues and skills. Depending on the goals of the session, possible activities during the core conversation may include: analyzing a skill or project; teaching or demonstrating a skill; sharing information or techniques; brainstorming obstacles or solutions; discussing current behavior; or clarifying the need for adjustments in behavior.

- *Consider learning preferences.* Think about how you can show or model a skill (for a visual learner), describe or discuss techniques (for an auditory learner), or involve the employee in some tangible action (for a kinesthetic learner). (See page 101.)

- *Clarify SMART goals together.* At this stage, both parties should work on establishing and agreeing on future SMART goals (discussed on pages 98–99.)

**Step 5: Closing the session:**   The close of the session provides an opportunity for you to reinforce the main messages of the meeting.

- *Summarize the session.* Using your paraphrasing skills and ability to synthesize, highlight key elements of the session. Note mutually agreed-upon goals and an action plan for achieving them, including follow-up strategy and next steps. Be very clear: use specific language and avoid vague words or unclear time requirements. Finally, offer coaching or training opportunities to address areas needing improvement.

- *Ask the employee to recap.* Ask the employee to recap strengths and areas for improvement, since verbalizing helps reinforce perceptions and improves commitment to goals.

- *End on a positive note.* Recognize the employee's progress and accomplishments and offer encouragement and support. Your enthusiasm for the process is an important motivator.

**Step 6: Following up and coaching on the job:**   Maintain frequent contact with your employee so you can provide timely feedback and reinforce her efforts.

- *Keep in touch.* Coaching continues through follow-up sessions and, most importantly, through timely feedback. Try to schedule frequent and regular sessions. If scheduling is a challenge, try for brief conversations or phone calls to stay in touch. Share and discuss obstacles, and modify goals as necessary.

- *Keep records.* Since perceptions are selective and faulty, we tend to remember the big mistakes or the unusual and most recent happenings more than the standard day-to-day events. Remember to keep regular records of events relating to the areas of coaching to avoid this memory pitfall.

- *Create and maintain a coaching grid.* One possible way to facilitate record-keeping is with a coaching grid of the sort shown on the next page. Along the top of the grid, write specific, agreed-upon areas of development corresponding to SMART objectives. Down the side are units of time that might correspond to coaching blocks—days, weeks, or months. Within each of the blocks of the matrix, jot brief examples of successes (+) or problems (−) in each of those areas. Developing this grid should be a joint effort between the coach and the person being coached, and both people should keep a copy.

    Keep a copy of the grid in an easily accessible spot, so notes can be made as close to the experience as possible. If both you and the employee keep records, you can use the grid to compare results, track progress, and determine when objectives have either been achieved or should be adjusted.

| **COACHING GRID** | | | |
|---|---|---|---|
| Go beyond the numbers | Respond quickly to written requests | Bend for team | Manage meetings |
| October | | | |
| November | | | |
| December | | | |
| January | | | |

*SOURCE:* L. Russell, Professional Development Company

---

In summary, successful performance appraisals are based on your willingness to view them as coaching opportunities. Plan to integrate the building block interpersonal skills of listening and feedback, questioning and responding skills, and social style awareness. In addition, set effective objectives and think of how to achieve them. Finally, perfect your abilities by creating a well-structured and complete session and a follow-up plan.

# Bibliography

Argyris, Chris, *On Organizational Learning*, 2nd ed. Malden, MA: Blackwell Business, 1999.

Black, James M., *How to Get Results from Interviewing*. New York: McGraw-Hill, 1970.

Bolton, Robert, *People Skills: How to Assert Yourself, Listen to Others, and Resolve Conflicts*. New York: Simon & Schuster, 1986.

Bolton, Robert and Dorothy Grover Bolton, *People Styles at Work*. New York: American Management Association, 1996.

————, *Social Style/Management Style*. New York: American Management Association, 1984.

Cialdini, Robert, *Influence: The Psychology of Persuasion*. New York: Quill William Morrow, 1993.

————, "Harnessing the Science of Persuasion." *Harvard Business Review*, October 2001.

Coleman, Daniel, *Working with Emotional Intelligence*. New York: Bantam Books, 1998.

Fisher, Roger and William Ury, *Getting to Yes*. New York: Penguin Books, 1991.

Hall, Edward, *Beyond Culture*. New York: Doubleday, 1989.

Lewicki, Roy J., David M. Saunders, and John W. Minton. *Negotiation,* 3rd ed. Boston: Irwin McGraw Hill, 1999.

Merrill, David W. and Roger H. Reid, *Personal Styles and Effective Performance*. Radnor, PA: Chilton Book Company, 1981.

Munter, Mary, *Guide to Managerial Communication*, 6th ed. Upper Saddle River, NJ: Prentice Hall, 2003.

Richmond, Virginia P. and James C. McCroskey, *Nonverbal Behavior in Interpersonal Relations,* 4th ed. Boston: Allyn and Bacon, 2000.

Stewart, John and Carole Logan, *Together: Communicating Interpersonally,* 4th ed. New York: McGraw-Hill, Inc., 1993.

Thompson, Leigh, *The Mind and Heart of the Negotiator.* Upper Saddle River, NJ: Prentice Hall, 1998.

Trenholme, Sarah, *Thinking through Communication,* 2nd ed. Boston: Allyn and Bacon, 1999.

———— and Arthur Jensen, *Interpersonal Communication.* Belmont, CA: Wadsworth Publishing Company, 2000.

Wall, Bob, *Working Relationships.* Palo Alto, CA: Davies-Black, 1999.

Yate, Martin John, *Hiring the Best.* Boston: Bob Adams, Inc., 1987.

————, *Knock 'em Dead,* 4th ed. Holbrook, MA: Bob Adams, Inc., 1990.

# Index